Timeless Deja Vu: A Paranormal Personal History

By Bruce Olav Solheim, Ph.D.

Illustrations by

Gary Dumm

Copyright © 2019 Bruce Olav Solheim

ISBN: 978-0-578-46446-6

Boots to Books
Glendora, CA 91741 USA

bootstobooks@gmail.co
www.bootstobooks.com

D0770211

TIMELESS

DEJA VU

A PARANORMAL PERSONAL HISTORY

by Bruce Olav Solheim, Ph.D.

Illustrations by Gary Dumm

BB
BOOTS
TO
BOOKS

ACKNOWLEDGEMENTS

I would like to thank God, my spirit guides Theodora and Ozzie, and all my spirit friends, especially Gene and Maia. I'd also like to thank Citrus College for letting me teach my paranormal personal history class, super engineer Scotty Z. at Artistfirst.com radio, Coast to Coast AM with George Noory, Conan O'Brien, David Willson, my girl Ginger, my friends Dr. E.M. Young, Dr. Terje Simonsen, Terry Lovelace, Dr. Dean Radin, my life coach Heather Heselton, and my psychic advisor Sheena Metal. Last, but not least, I want to thank my history and paranormal students, my family, my mother the psychic, my father the skeptic, my talented editor George Verongos, and my friend and illustrator extraorinaire, Gary Dumm.

Just as a reminder to my readers, the stories in this book reflect my recollection of events. Some names, locations, and identifying characteristics have been changed to protect the privacy of those depicted. Dialogue has been re-created from memory.

TABLE OF CONTENTS

PROLOGUE

I've got a guardian angel. It may be true that many people believe that they have one, but my mom told me that I had one, and I've witnessed the work of my guardian angel, so I know I have one. Experience is better than belief. I don't always rely on my guardian angel's intervention on my behalf, but I certainly welcome it when it happens. I can't really describe what she looks like; I think of light, pure energy, and so beautiful as to be beyond description. I'll use the female pronoun, but I don't think guardian angels have a gender. I know her name though, it's Theodora. This book, in fact, was inspired by my guardian angel Theodora. When I was born, my godfather, Uncle Einar, gave me a teddy bear. I always called that teddy bear, Teddy, but I really didn't think of Teddy as being male or female. In the 1980s, Teddy was left outside and rotted. He was ruined and had to be thrown away. Last year, I found a teddy bear on eBay that looked just like Teddy and was the same vintage (1958). I bought the teddy bear, and Teddy sits behind me on my bookshelf as I write these words. I now know that Teddy is actually Theodora—an earthly representation of my guardian angel. She will always be with me.

Picking up from the first *Timeless* book, we'll explore various paranormal phenomena that I've experienced (ghosts, hauntings, precognition, aliens, and others) in *Timeless Deja Vu*. Now that I've received feedback from the readers of the first book, I can incorporate their thoughtful suggestions into this sequel. I've also started teaching a Paranormal Personal History course through community education at Citrus College. The first class had 35 students from all walks of life. They were indeed a diverse, fascinating, intelligent, and fun group of people. Gary Dumm has once again lent his enormous talent to illustrating this second book.

I know in my first *Timeless* book I said that I could not contact people's dead relatives, but apparently, I can. In fact, I had been practicing mediumship randomly since I was four years old. No wonder I felt comfortable in graveyards when I was a kid. Much of the paranormal deals with what happens after death. I've gathered some quotes about this topic that can serve as a starting point for discussion. Let's begin with Carl Jung. "What happens after death is so unspeakably glorious that our imagination and our feelings do not suffice to form even an approximate conception of it. The dissolution of our time-bound form in eternity brings no loss of meaning." I'm intrigued by Jung's explanation. I'm particularly interested in what he means by "...the dissolution of our time-bound form in eternity." In other words, we're timeless, just as my friend Gene Thorkildsen told me after his death.

And then there is Plato in *The Apology*. "No one knows whether death may not be the greatest of all blessings for a man, yet men fear it as if they knew that it is the greatest of evils." In the first book, I wrote a story about my near-death at Deception Pass, Washington. I experienced a fork in the road of time. I suggested that perhaps death, as we the living understand it, is the greatest deception of all. If we live in fear of death, we're not really living.

The next quote is from American writer Henry Miller. "Of course, you don't die. Nobody dies. Death does not exist. You only reach a new level of vision, a new realm of consciousness, a new unknown world." Miller doesn't mince words. There is no death. Our consciousness, which most scientists have great difficulty explaining without dipping their toes into the paranormal realm, isn't extinguished, it lives on. We may not yet understand how or why, but my own experience is enough to convince me. If we consider non-local consciousness (consciousness existing independent of the brain and the body) based on scientific evidence as being real and on the leading edge of science, what can we do with that idea? Dr. Dean Radin, chief scientist at the Institute for Noetic Sciences (IONS), has a suggestion in his latest book, *Real Magic: Ancient Wisdom, Modern Science, and a Guide to the Secret Power of the Universe*. He writes about the esoteric traditions going back to shamanism and discovers that for our ancestors who practiced this philosophy, consciousness was fundamental, and consciousness comes before time and space. "If that is true, it means that our esoteric ideas about magic are also true," according to Radin.

Radin holds that magic involves three basic components: divination, force of will, and theurgy. Divination is the ability to see at a distance through space and time. Force of will is the idea that a person's intention can move things in our world. Theurgy (from the Greek, meaning God-work) is the belief that there are intelligent spirits that we can interact with and that can work on our behalf and can also possess you and do evil things. He points out that magicians believe that magic is real but feel that science is incapable of learning about magic. Religion acknowledges that magic is real but dictates that only the clergy can perform magic and everyone else who does is demonic and heretical. Science contends that magic is just superstition, doesn't work, and we already got rid of it long ago. Radin says that all three traditions are wrong. Scientists can study divination (precognition, clairvoyance), force of will (psychokinesis), and theurgy (spirit mediums and near-death experience). He believes the core ideas of esoteric magic are probably true. Radin has support in the science world. Dr. Brian Josephson, Nobel Laureate in Physics and Emeritus Professor of Physics at the University of Cambridge wrote about *Real Magic*: "A thought-provoking book. The author makes a convincing case for the reality and significance of magic."

And finally, there is an incredible Inupiat (Eskimo) proverb. "Perhaps they are not stars, but rather openings in heaven where the love of our lost ones pours through and shines down upon us to let us know they are happy." I like this explanation most of all because it ties in the entangled universe, non-local consciousness, and our families. All of us are connected through the past, fleeting present, and the future. For this book, I've stuck my neck out a bit more, and hopefully you, my dear readers, will find *Timeless Deja Vu* even more meaningful than *Timeless*. Thank you for your open minds and hearts, and always remember that you're the hero or heroine of your own life story.

DEJA VIEW (1967)

Deja vu, the phenomenon of having the feeling that the present situation you're experiencing has already happened in the past, is something I've had my whole life. Sometimes the feeling is intense, other times it's minimal and fleeting. I've noticed that my deja vu experiences have diminished as I've grown older, both in intensity and frequency. There are several fascinating theories concerning deja vu.

One theory holds that the experience of deja vu is tied to sensory context. A sight or smell could trigger our subconscious to remember a similar situation. Another theory suggests that as we transfer information from short-term to long-term memory, it creates a temporary illusion that we've experienced something before. Still another theory is based on familiarity recognition. In this case, deja vu is a result of recognizing something when we only have a faint memory of this thing or person or situation that is somewhat similar to the current situation. This vague memory can't provide us with the details of who, what, where, when, how, and why. The hologram theory holds that one element (i.e., a sound or smell) can remind you of a previous memory and then our brains create a three-dimensional image, like a hologram, to make us feel like we're reliving the same event. The divided attention theory suggests that deja vu is caused by us recognizing something received subconsciously. In other words, deja vu is due to a subliminal recognition of something. Accordingly, our subconscious is aware but our conscious mind isn't. Many believe that these subliminal messages could come from the internet, television, and social media.

Others think that the amygdala, a small region of our brain responsible for emotion and fear, causes temporary disorientation in dangerous situations that have similarity to previous frightening events which could then account for deja vu. Many scientists subscribe to a recent theory that deja vu is merely the frontal regions of the brain checking through our memories and alerting us to some memory error. In other words, a conflict between what we've actually experienced and

5

what we think we've experienced. They believe that deja vu is a sign that your brain's memory checking system is operational. Some even say that deja vu is related to dissociative identity disorder and schizophrenia.

There are also less clinical and more ambitious and imaginative theories. The parallel universe theory contends that deja vu is a momentary crossover with a parallel universe. In other words, a parallel version of you may have done the same thing as you in a parallel universe, and you have a memory of that action. Another fascinating theory is that deja vu is remembering a precognitive dream. For instance, countless people around the world (including me) reported strange dreams relating to 9/11 before those tragic events unfolded. A few theorists believe that reincarnation could account for deja vu. Recognizing a particular sound, smell, or image from our prior existence causes us to remember this previous life and make it feel like we're reliving the past in the present. Finally, we come to the infinite realities theory that most closely resembles what I believe. With this theory, deja vu is a remarkable event that wakes us up from our artificially created realities. What if the past, present, and future are all happening simultaneously, as my friend Gene Thorkildsen tried to explain to me after his death. Deja vu could be a glimpse of other realities; a slip or crack in time and space.

I believe that overly simple or clinical explanations don't take into account the complexity of deja vu experiences and tend to dismiss subjective experience. My most intense deja vu experiences have included specific places, people, situations, words, smells, sounds, and many other details. My theory is a wave theory. Imagine time as a wave, the crest of the wave curls and overlaps the trough. The space between the edge of the crest (the event horizon) and the point of inward curl of the trough is where deja vu occurs. Here is my crude illustration:

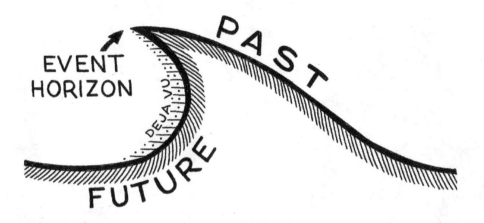

Based on my personal experience, I don't believe that deja vu is my brain playing tricks on me or some false-positive check system for memory. Deja vu is our ability to glimpse the infinite. As New York Yankees Hall of Fame catcher Yogi Berra once said. "It's like deja vu all over again." Not surprisingly, some scientists and mental health professionals, the so-called experts, and professional skeptics unite in their opposition to anything paranormal. It's like this has all happened before.

THE BAD BOYS AND GIRLS (1969)

My brother was fighting in the Vietnam War in 1969. He wrote home about how the Viet Cong set up booby traps to kill American soldiers. I loved to play army in the woods with my friends Johnny and Tommy, and I kept them informed about what my brother was doing in Vietnam. When we played war at home, we also set up booby traps around our tree forts, just in case the bad boys and girls came. The bad boys and girls were kids who lived on the hill above us. I'm not sure why they always attacked our forts and stole our precious items. I didn't even know their names, but you don't have to know someone's name to hate them and make them an enemy.

One day in that summer of 1969, we noticed that the bad boys and girls built a fort near our part of the woods. There wasn't any clear boundary between our part of the woods and theirs, but we still seemed to know intrinsically where our territory ended and theirs began. Their fort appeared to be a little too close for comfort. We decided to break into their fort and conduct some sabotage. Once we got into the plywood and junk-ridden structure about ten feet up into a tree, we saw all sorts of items. There were dirty magazines, cigarettes, beer, a bottle of whiskey, and other naughty things. We took all the stuff and put it in a pillowcase and left. We gave it all to Johnny and Tommy's father. He said he would smoke the cigarettes, drink the beer and whiskey, and burn up the magazines. Tommy told me that it took his father a lot longer to get rid of those magazines than it took him to smoke the cigarettes and drink the beer and whiskey.

We should have figured that our raid on their fort would result in retaliation on their part. One war always leads to another. I had a dream where I was lost in the woods and could not find my way home. Terrible dark things were lurking in the shadows and were threatening me. I woke up before I knew what was in the shadows. A few weeks after our raiding party, we had a war with the bad boys and girls. Their fort was reinforced and stocked with rocks and dirt bombs. Our fort wasn't that far away from theirs. They started the war by throwing some rocks against the side of our fort and yelling at us. We used sling shots to fire back. My friend Tommy got hit in the head with a rock, but it didn't seem to affect him very much. He usually acted like he had been hit in the head with a rock anyway. The battle lasted only ten minutes and then someone's mom yelled that lunch was ready. We all headed home. Maybe they should have let all the moms show up in Vietnam and yell for everyone to come home and eat. You never know, it could have worked.

A few weeks later, we were playing our usual army game in the woods. We wandered a bit further into the woods looking for cool new battle areas. We went a lot further than any of us had ever gone before; we encountered unfamiliar terrain with no useful landmarks. We lost sight of our territory and neighborhood. Then, out of the blue, the bad boys and girls ambushed us. They must have followed us deep into the woods. It was probably to get us back for raiding their fort. Johnny, Tommy, and I were all captured. They were bigger than us, so we could not do anything. They made us march up and down in a muddy ravine filled with old junk and boards with rusty nails that stuck out. I was scared but acted like a good little soldier and told my buddies that we would get away when the bad boys and girls weren't looking. They made us march even farther away. They tied us up and tortured us, and I was even hit in the head and blacked out. I wasn't sure at the time, but I thought that one of the older boys had done something terrible to me. But then our break came. One of the bad boys and girls had cigarettes and offered them to the others. Once they were distracted with that, I told my friends to run and don't look back. We ran, and ran, and ran some more. Finally, we made it back to our part of the woods. We learned a valuable lesson that day, never go into unfamiliar territory and always stay alert and prepared.

I never asked Johnny or Tommy to confirm what happened, and I didn't tell my parents or anyone else after the incident in the woods. I was too confused and embarrassed. In therapy, many years later, I finally dealt with the fact that I had suffered sexual abuse as a child.

The realization hit me one evening when I was fighting with a particularly severe panic attack. The bad boys and girls who captured Johnny, Tommy, and myself when we wandered too far into the woods while playing army, had sexually abused me. My violence towards others may have emanated from this. But I didn't want to be a victim, and I didn't want to be a victimizer. I seemed to be locked into a downward spiral. My doubts about my conduct during the abuse made me question my self-worth. I learned that children were not equipped to deal with sexual situations. Also, I had been powerless and unconscious. I had no voice. Before I was abused, I was a vital, gregarious, class clown. After I was sexually assaulted, I was withdrawn, brooding, moody, and prone to violent outbursts. I gained a lot of weight, as I found solace in food. But the ridicule I was subjected to by my classmates for being fat attacked this sanctuary of food that I had created.

I began looking back at how this traumatic event had changed my life. I remembered that Timmy, a good friend from age six to thirteen, lived in the country. I used to stay overnight at his house and he would stay overnight with me sometimes. One day, I called him to see if I could come over. He put the phone down and went to ask his mom. I could hear them in the background as he was asking her if I could come over.

"I don't want that strange little fat boy over here this weekend," she said. My friend returned to the phone and told me that he could not have guests over. I said that was okay and that I would talk to him later. His mom had always smiled at me and was nice. I could not understand why she would be so angry and mean. I was totally crushed. I never saw my friend again. Most of my friendships ended under similarly abrupt circumstances.

I've acknowledged having suffered childhood sexual abuse. I'm still working through unresolved anger, shame, frightening dreams, anxiety, and depression. The only positive thing that I think came from this horrible experience is that it may have enhanced my creative and paranormal abilities. I also realized how my childhood mini-version of war was like real war. We feel compelled to find enemies, inflame feelings of hatred, and wage war. This cycle of war goes on endlessly. Pretend soldiers become real soldiers. Pretend wars become real wars. My premonition of the experience in the woods so many years ago was a warning. I no longer let such warnings go unheeded.

READING MINDS IN OREGON (1971)

In the Summer of 1971, I was camping with my parents on the Oregon coast. I've always loved camping. My mom said that my first camping trip was in 1959, and I wasn't even walking yet. She said I was filthy from crawling around the campsite. I love the smells of camping: the wood fire, the outside cooking, the pine and fir trees, the cool crisp air in the morning, and the animals looking for handouts. One night after dinner, my mom came out of the camper with a deck of cards. Dad lit the gas lantern, and he had already built a raging fire in the fire pit, as usual. My mom sat on the opposite side of the table and pulled out a card and stared at it closely.

"Guess what card I have," she said. My dad got up to put more logs on the fire. I looked at my mom and looked at the back of the card trying to picture the suit first, then the number or face.

"The eight of hearts," I said. My mom turned over the card and sure enough, it was the eight of hearts. My dad was unimpressed.

"See, Asbjørn," she said to Dad, "we can read minds." My father turned around and smiled.

"Lucky guess," he said.

"Try again," Mom said as she drew out another card and concentrated carefully. Once again, I pictured the suit first. I saw clubs but had trouble seeing the number. Then, it came to me; it wasn't a number.

"Jack of clubs!" I blurted out. Dad walked over and looked at the card as my mom put it down on the picnic table.

"That's right," she said, as she looked defiantly at Dad.

"Luck again," he said, but with less enthusiasm and certainty, and maybe a little worried as well.

Mom gave me the deck of cards. I paused for a moment to look at the nearly full moon and stars glimmering above the tall trees. I could hear the ocean waves breaking in the distance and smell the salty sea breeze.

"You try to send, and I'll guess," she said. I took the deck and picked a card. The same process, I concentrated on the suit first, and then the number or face. I picked the ten of diamonds.

"Ok, guess," I said. My mom closed her eyes and thought for a long time in silence.

"It's a red card…a number…ten of hearts," she said. I threw the card down on the picnic table.

"Close," I said.

"But it was a ten of diamonds," Dad said as he shook his head and smiled.

"Try one more time, and then I'll believe it," he said.

I took out another card and concentrated. The five of clubs.

"Put the card back on top of the deck," Dad said. I put the card back on top of the deck and placed the deck on the picnic table. Mom closed her eyes and concentrated.

"A black card," she said. She concentrated some more, and so did I.

"Not a number, it's an ace," she said with confidence. We all waited for her to specify the suit.

"Spades?" she asked. My dad turned over the top card on the deck. It was a five of clubs. He looked satisfied.

"That's wrong," he said smiling as he put the card back on the deck, but it slid off and fell between the cracks in the table.

"At least it was a black card," I said as I started to bend down to retrieve the card.

"Yeah," my mom said. Dad just smiled and shook his head again.

"One more time, Bruce, you guess again," she said. I raised up again in anticipation.

"No, that's enough," Dad said. He was serious, and when Dad got serious, I listened.

"Leave it be, no sense doing anymore," he warned.

"Why?" I asked. My mom then nodded in agreement with my father.

"Your father is right," she said. I was wondering why, but I didn't say anything else.

Dad started carving with his buck knife, and Mom went back to the camper to clean some dishes, as I sat and stared at the cards. A distant fog horn sounded its lonely call. Then I remembered that the card had slipped under the table. As I leaned over to look, I noticed that there were two cards under the table; I grabbed them. One card was the five of clubs and the other was the ace of spades, the card that my mom had guessed. The ace must have slipped through one of the spaces between the wood on the picnic table like the other card. I sat up and quietly pushed the cards back into the deck and didn't say anything; I didn't want to make Dad upset. There was silence, except for the on-shore wind and the breakers on the beach. What did it mean? At the time I wasn't sure. All that I knew was that I could see the card my mom was thinking of clearly in my mind and she could do likewise. How? My mom and I had a telepathic connection and she was training me and preparing me for who I am today.

FOUR-LEAF CLOVERS (1972)

When I was thirteen, I joined the Civil Air Patrol (CAP). My brother's participation in the Vietnam War sparked my interest in the military. We wore Air Force-like uniforms and had rank, but the primary function of the CAP was search and rescue operations for downed pilots and airplanes. We would meet once a week at the old American Legion Hall in Bothell. I can still remember walking past the World War II veterans sitting on red leather barstools at the long, dark wooden bar drinking their scotch and sodas and smoking Lucky Strike cigarettes pinched between their yellow-nailed fingers. Rat Pack music played on their Radio Shack hi-fi. They stared at us with deeply anguished eyes, unblinking. Perhaps they saw themselves in our youthful enthusiasm and innocence. Maybe they sensed that loss. They realized that it stood in sharp contrast to their current hard-boiled worldview after fighting and watching men die in battle. Our advisor was an Air Force sergeant named Mike. He would yell at us; we would march, stand in formation, and then study aviation and leadership topics. I would find out later that this was excellent preparation for the real military.

Mike was mean to most of us, but he had his favorites. He especially liked the two young girls we had in our unit. One weekend, we went out on a bivouac to Moses Lake. There I met other CAP cadets from all over Washington, but I was lonely because my friend was sick and couldn't come on the bivouac, so I was with people I didn't know. One morning, I was admiring a clover patch near my tent in our uni's area. The morning dew and soft sunlight made the clovers into a shimmering carpet. It was like an ant's forest I thought. I've always loved clovers. Since I was a little boy, I had searched for four-leaf clovers, but I never found any. As I was searching through the clover patch, one of the older cadets who outranked me came up and positioned himself right in front of me. He stepped on the clovers.

"Don't you salute authority, cadet?" he asked.

"I'm sorry sir, I didn't see you coming," I said as I rendered a hand salute. He took his swagger stick that he was carrying and hit me in the head knocking my hat off. It hurt, and I was trying not to cry.

"You are a stupid, fat little piece of shit, don't piss me off anymore or I'll have you doing details for the whole weekend," he barked. He then pivoted on the clover patch and tore it apart as he left. I sat there in silence once again trying not to cry or reveal my real feelings. Why did I come here? Why didn't I stand up to that bully? Later, we played capture the flag and then the rest of the time Sergeant Mike used all of us to hand out election fliers door to door for a friend of his who was running for office. He made us work an entire day without a break and without lunch or anything to drink.

Years later, I was camping with my girlfriend Charlotte at Vashon Island State Park in Washington State. She had driven into town for some supplies. It was early in the morning, and the sun shone on the clover patch by our tent. I thought about that mean boy so many years ago, and what he did and what he said. I let it hurt my feelings for years, but no more. Why didn't I report that asshole cadet? I didn't have to take such abuse. And I'm sure that Sergeant Mike would have been punished had the CAP known that he was using cadets for election purposes. But they were gone, nowhere near this perfect clover patch. It had been my lifelong goal to find a four-leaf clover. Then, remarkably, I saw a different pattern out of the corner of my eye. Could it be? There to my right was a beautiful four-leaf clover. Its leaves were intact as well. A lifelong mission accomplished.

On average, there is only one four-leaf clover for every 10,000 three-leaf clovers, and no clover plants naturally produce four-leaf clovers—it's a mutation. That is why they are so rare. The leaves of a four-leaf clover stand for faith, hope, love, and luck. In the Irish tradition, the Shamrock or three-leaf clover represents the Holy Trinity: The Father, The Son, and The Holy Ghost. The fourth leaf represents God's grace. I figured that by taking my time to see, not to look or search, I could find a four-leaf clover finally. Or did I? Perhaps by seeing the patterns, the very rhythm of nature, the four-leaf clover found me. Since that time, when I'm walking, I occasionally stop for no apparent reason, look down, and there it is—a four-leaf clover. They find me all the time now. I've even found a five-leaf and a six-leaf clover. There is only one five-leaf clover for every one million three-leaf clovers. I'm not sure what the odds are for finding a six-leaf clover. Maybe I hear them calling to me subconsciously in a nearly silent whisper. Finding me, I rejoice in the four-leaf clover's simplicity, complexity, beauty, and power. It has always been there, waiting. My paranormal abilities were developing. Perhaps by finally having faith in myself, I developed confidence through my experiences, gained love through learning to love others honestly, and made my own luck in the end.

TROLL ISLAND (1972)

During a performance of my World War II play *The Epiphany* in Norway in 2016, I met my old friend Per Sture and his mother. I hadn't seen his mother since 1972, and I hadn't seen Per Sture since 2003 when I lived in Tromsø. In tears, he told me that his daughter was one of the 77 young people killed in 2011 when Norwegian far-right extremist Anders Breivik went on his murderous rampage in Oslo and Utøya in Norway. It was the deadliest attack in Norway since the Nazi invasion in 1940. I can't even imagine Per Sture's burden of grief. I sometimes wish that I could travel in time and warn people of tragic events to come. I know that such warnings and prevention of events could alter the future and maybe cause even worse outcomes and problems, at least according to theorists. I've also heard it said that to save one life is to save all of humanity. I don't know for sure, but I think I would take a chance to save a life; theorists be damned.

In 1972, my parents and I visited some relatives on Langøya, near our family home on Andøya in Northern Norway. We spent a few days with my sixteen-year-old cousin Per Sture and his family. At least I thought he was my cousin. Later we found out that we weren't directly related. During our visit in 1972, Per Sture told me that we were taking a boat trip out to the small island where they had a cabin. The fjord was very narrow, and the water was calm where they lived. We set out in the tiny motorboat and passed by a tall but small island. It had a few cabins on it.

"Is that where you have your cabin?" I asked.

"Oh no, that is Troll Island," Per Sture said very matter-of-factly.

"Troll Island? You mean trolls live there?" I asked.

"Oh yes," Per Sture said.

"Do they live in those little cabins?" I asked.

"I think so," he said. I thought for a moment; then I had a theory.

"Maybe they're not trolls…people in the past could've left crippled and deformed babies outside to die because of superstition or because they couldn't work on the farms or fish. Then, maybe those babies were picked up by other crippled and deformed people and taken to the island," I said with great excitement.

"Sure," Per Sture said unenthusiastically. I was intrigued by my theory and the thought of exploring the island.

"Let's go visit them," I foolishly blurted out.

"Are you crazy, Bruce? They don't care for us much, we leave them alone, and they leave us alone," he said.

"Well lets at least go a little closer so I can see better," I said as I squinted to see any sign of the trolls.

"Best to keep our distance," Per Sture warned.

What if I had traveled back in time and my thirteen-year-old self could have cautioned Per Sture not to allow his daughter to stay on Utøya on July 22, 2011. He might have thought I was crazy, but would he remember? Would he tell his daughter not to go on that outing? Would his daughter and 76 other people still be alive? But I wasn't a time traveler, and we kept going, slowly making our way through the fjord, the tiny island growing further away with each chug, chug, chug of the old boat motor, unaware of what future lay ahead of us.

MY NAZI AUNT (1973)

Not everyone has a Nazi aunt. And I'm not talking about some phony neo-Nazi, skinhead type. I'm talking about a real Nazi. During World War II, my dad's youngest sister chose to collaborate with the Germans after they invaded Norway on April 9, 1940. My father was put into a labor camp by the Nazis, and his eldest brother Thorvald was stationed in England where he became a convoy commander ferrying supplies across the Atlantic to the British. He was sunk twice by German U-boats and survived. Uncle Thorvald was a war hero. Aunt Walborg was a war criminal.

My mom and dad didn't like to talk about my dad's youngest sister, Walborg. It was a sore subject. It's typical of that World War II generation to not talk about feelings and such things. But there was something more. My mom didn't like her, but I wasn't sure why. Walborg was born in 1920 in our family farm home in Åse, on the island of Andøya, in Northern Norway. She was the youngest of five siblings. The eldest was Thorvald, then Astrid, then my dad Asbjørn, then Solbjørg, and last, Walborg. I met her the first time when we took the Stavangerfjord across the Atlantic in 1962 and traveled through Oslo to Andøya to live with my dad's mother. I barely remember Aunt Walborg from that trip, but apparently, we stayed with her and Uncle Ragnar in Oslo.

In the Summer of 1972, I returned to Norway with my parents. My grandmother had just died, and my father was entangled in a legal struggle with my cousin Eva over the property and home in Åse. We stayed with Aunt Walborg and Uncle Ragnar in Oslo, so my father could meet with an attorney. I remember that Walborg was very nice to us and made great food, but I also noticed a tension between my mom and her. By this time, I had picked up on little bits and pieces of the story about my aunt. I knew that she had picked the wrong side in World War II, but I wasn't sure why and there were no significant details available to me.

Aunt Walborg came to visit us in Seattle in 1973 when I was 15 years old. It was Christmas time. It was probably because my pubescent hormones were beginning to rage, but that was the first time that I had noticed how attractive she was. Aunt Walborg was 51 years old, but she looked at least ten years younger and had a very shapely physique. She was always perfectly coiffured and wore expensive and tight-fitting dresses. Aunt Walborg was like a movie star. Her husband, Uncle Ragnar, looked like Richard Burton. She had a mystique about her, and they made quite a handsome couple. Unfortunately, Walborg and Ragnar liked to drink to excess. I noticed that they got drunk every night, much to the displeasure of my mother. I also noticed how my aunt looked at me as she elegantly pushed a cigarette to her red lips and inhaled. And then, still gazing at me with glistening dark brown eyes, she slowly exhaled the smoke which enveloped her and framed her petite, pretty face. I could not take my eyes off her. She had an allure, and the fact that she had been a Nazi added to her mystique. Walborg and Ragnar had a bedroom upstairs in our home in Seattle, and I had the downstairs bedroom.

After Christmas, shortly before they were to leave to go back to Norway, I woke up to find Walborg in my room. I could smell her perfume and see her in the shadows. I was aroused and breathing heavily. My blankets were pulled to the side. Although I didn't know for sure, I had the feeling that she had been in my bed and that we had had sexual contact. I know that I had been dreaming about being surrounded by people watching me having sex with a girl, but I thought it was just a strange dream, not real. The people were not ordinary people; they were little, and not quite human. Walborg was a very slight woman, maybe five feet tall and barely 100 pounds, so it was possible for her to slip into my bed undetected and accomplish this while I slept. I had never had sex before, so it was all new to me, but I could smell her all over me and in the bed sheets. I felt like I couldn't move—frozen in the bed. Then, before I could say anything, she was gone, never uttering a word. As I sit here typing these words 45 years later, and without going into details that would better be suited for the editorial pages of *Hustler* magazine, I know exactly what happened. I believe that these little people were of alien origin and they had something to do with my Nazi aunt and the sexual contact I had with her.

In 1975, two years after my sexual encounter with my Nazi aunt, I continued to have weird dreams about these little beings and my aunt, and I began to be able to perform incredible physical feats. I've vague memories of small shadowy figures entering my basement room; sometimes it was sexual, sometimes not. I remember waking up in the middle of the night once, and I was outside, in the woods by my house. How did I get there? Then I remembered that I was able to run through the woods by my house in complete darkness at an incredible rate of speed without bumping into anything or falling, it was like I could fly through the woods. I could run and leap over any fence and even leap up on to my brother's garage roof—he lived in a little house below us on the hill. I felt invincible and like I had superpowers. I used to be afraid of the dark, but I increasingly came to feel that I was one with the darkness. This wasn't good.

We stayed with my aunt again in 1975 on a stopover traveling to Northern Norway. I was with my parents, and I don't remember anything unusual happening. I learned more of the details concerning Walborg's activities during World War II from my cousins. Aunt Walborg gave me $600 to buy a car (a 1966 Triumph Spitfire) a year later in 1976, something my mom and dad were not happy about. It could have been money to silence me or as a reward or who knows why? Writing about this incident with my aunt and thinking back to the demonic experience in 1978 that I wrote about in the first *Timeless* book, "Hell is Empty," I now believe that the demonic experience might have been an alien contact and attempted abduction. Mrs. Burns, whom I thought was a witch, may have represented something non-terrestrial as well. The column of fire in an arc over my head was perhaps a portal they wanted to use to transport me away. I remember the voice emanating from the column of fire. Recently, during one of my meditation connections, I asked my spirit guides and friends in the spirit world, and they told me that the incident was both demonic and alien.

"Both?" I asked.

"Yes, it was both," they said in unison.

"What do you mean by both?" I asked.

"Mrs. Burns was tied into evil demonic things and the Reptilians," they said, again in unison.

"So, the aliens, these Reptilians, they didn't abduct me, but they tried?" I asked to clarify. I then saw my spirit guide protector Ozzie, the warrior, arms crossed, silently smiling.

"Ozzie was there to help," said my other spirit guide Theodora, "so they couldn't, but they tried for sure."

In 1978, I joined the Army, and after being sent to West Germany, I went AWOL, a story that I also documented in the first *Timeless* book. My aunt didn't know that I was coming to Oslo and was quite surprised when I called her and Uncle Ragnar from the train station. They were both nice to me, and I remember my uncle making crude sexual jokes and even wetting his finger and pretending to poke it into my aunt's backside when she had her back to him standing on a stool and retrieving a satchel from the closet in their hallway. I laughed, and my aunt turned around and smiled seductively at me and told him to stop it. She gave me the satchel that belonged to my grandfather Albert. They helped convince me to return to West Germany and stick out my three-year overseas tour.

I saw Aunt Walborg again in 1992 when I was conducting doctoral research in Oslo. She had invited me to stay with her. Uncle Ragnar had just recently passed away, so she was living alone. At 72, she was still lovely and had maintained her shapely figure. My aunt took me shopping and bought me clothes and gifts. One day she got furious when I asked if I could stay a few nights with my cousin. Her anger wasn't something you wanted to endure for long. I gave in quickly and complied with her wishes, and all was peaceful again. She cooked for me, and we went out for dinner, and she kept telling me how handsome I was, and how fit I was and seemed always to be hovering nearby as I wrote research notes and read in my little room. I would catch her fixing her stare on me, and I felt this odd compulsion just to grab her into my arms and take her to bed and make love to her. But, how could I? She was my aunt and 38 years older than me. I fought those urges, but the signals were clear that my aunt wouldn't object to my initiating that type of sexual activity, in fact, I thought, hadn't she been encouraging me to do so? She insisted that I use her private bathroom that had an elaborate hot water system that was probably state of the art in 1958. Ordinarily, I would use the shower upstairs, but her bathroom was just off of her bedroom. She would have her bra and panties hanging in the bathroom for me to see. As I bathed, I felt the sensation of her staring at me. Maybe she had a peephole, I'm not sure, but it was a strange feeling. I noticed a series of books on her bookshelf in her room emblazoned with swastikas. I didn't dare ask her about them. I visited my cousin Eva briefly one day when Walborg had to go to a medical appointment. It was then that I got the full story of my aunt's activities as a member of the Gestapo during World War II.

Aunt Walborg worked as a nurse's aide at the start of the war helping the Nazis in the northern part of Norway. She fell in love with a German officer who was later sent to the Eastern Front in Russia never to return. Heartbroken over the loss of her sweetheart, she snapped and joined the Gestapo in Oslo to seek revenge against those who would dare challenge the Germans. Speaking perfect German, she was rewarded with one of the nicest apartments in Oslo and given anything she wanted, cars, French wine and perfume, the finest clothes and furs, and jewelry. She worked directly for SS Colonel Siegfried Wolfgang Fehmer who headed the Gestapo in Oslo headquartered at Victoria Terrasse. Her job was to identify members of the Norwegian Resistance.

One of the more famous incidents was on November 13, 1944, in the Plass Café in Oslo. Aunt Walborg, who went by her Nazi name of Wally, had set up to meet two members of the Oslo Gang resistance group—Gregers Gram and Edvard Tallaksen.

She told them that some German deserters wanted to share information and help the Resistance. She identified Gram and Tallaksen to the Gestapo agents in the café and then excused herself to go to the restroom. Gram was shot dead in the subsequent shootout with the Gestapo and Tallaksen was wounded and captured. Tallaksen was later taken to Akershus Fortress after receiving medical treatment. He was tortured but was able to commit suicide to avoid revealing anything about his comrades in the Resistance. In total, Wally was responsible for the deaths of nine members of the Resistance.

After the war, my aunt was arrested as a war criminal and sentenced to death for collaborating with the enemy during the occupation. Thanks to Uncle Thorvald using all his money and his war hero status, my aunt's sentence was commuted to 20 years, and in 1950 she was released because of psychiatric problems. Shortly after that she met and married Ragnar, who, oddly enough, was a Norwegian military officer. She took his last name and was able to hide her identity. My sister said that Walborg and Ragnar fought like cats and dogs, but that Ragnar had a trump card. If they were out on the town and got into a nasty argument, he would simply say, "Should I tell everyone here who you are?" That would silence her. In 1995, while I was visiting up north, my dad told me that part of the reason they immigrated to America was because of Walborg. Now I knew the whole story. Had it not been for my Nazi aunt, I would have been a fisherman and potato farmer in Northern Norway.

After my daughter Caitlin was born in 1996, Walborg came to visit my father in Seattle. I saw her one more time at my father's funeral in 1999, which I wrote about in a story called "A Hero's Welcome Home" in the first *Timeless* book. In 2003, I received a Fulbright Professor position at the University of Tromsø in Northern Norway and broke off my relationship with my sister over issues related to our father's estate. I stayed in touch with Aunt Walborg and she finally convinced me to speak to my sister again in 2005. That is something I'm very grateful for. Not long after that, Aunt Walborg died. My cousin Eva's book came out detailing her war hero father's exploits (my Uncle Thorvald) and the wartime treachery of our Nazi aunt. The book was popular, and the national media interviewed Eva in Norway. My play, *The Epiphany*, which was performed in Los Angeles in 2015, and again in Northern Norway in 2016, was based on my family history during World War II. *The Epiphany* story was carried on Norwegian national TV. I like to think that Aunt Walborg sought forgiveness at the end of her life. I know that her doctor was from Africa and her nurses were Pakistani. In keeping with her Nazi indoctrinated ideology, my aunt tended to blame people of color for all the problems in Norway. From what my cousin Eva said, her doctor and nurses treated her with the utmost dignity and respect. Did she seek redemption? I hope so. With the World War II generation fading fast from this world, I now carry the story forward, and hopefully the lessons. Evil attracts evil, whether it's terrestrial or alien, and love and compassion are stronger than the forces of hate and darkness.

ROCK AND ROLL (1977)

Elvis Aaron Presley died on August 16, 1977, which was also my brother's birthday. On that day, my friends and I had decided to hike the Columbia River Gorge in Eastern Washington State not far from the little town of Vantage. I've done some crazy things in my life, but what I did on that hiking and camping trip took the cake. Coming from the west, we passed through Vantage, population 74, and crossed over the I-90 bridge to the eastside of the Columbia River. In the early 1900s there was a small ferry that took people, cars, and wagons across the Columbia at Vantage. In 1927, the 1640-foot bridge was opened. The original cantilever bridge was replaced by the current bridge in 1962. Because of the Wanapum Dam, the Columbia at that point is really called Wanapum Lake and is quite broad.

We exited off I-90 on to the Old Vantage Highway and headed to Frenchman Coulee and Echo Basin. We parked in a dirt parking lot that looked more like a turnaround. In those days you didn't need any special permission or parking passes. Our plan was to hike to Frenchman Coulee and Echo Basin, see the beautiful sites, then head to the rim overlooking the Columbia River (Wanapum Lake). At the rim we planned to camp and sleep under the stars. There wasn't a soul anywhere and it was peaceful and tranquil. As we hiked, we sang every old Elvis song we could think of in honor of the King of Rock and Roll. My particularly heartfelt rendition of Blue Christmas was greatly admired. Frenchman Coulee is a feature left behind by the Ice-Age floods. The floodwaters ate away the underlying rock layers. The sandy scrub landscape was surrounded by steep cliff walls and some lovely basalt columns.

When we arrived at the rim of the Columbia Gorge, we staked out a relatively flat campsite near the ledge. As we put our packs down and spread out our sleeping pads, I noticed a large boulder perched precariously on the edge of the rim that went straight down to the water several hundred feet below us. The boulder was the size of a small refrigerator. Using our compact camp stoves, we cooked some macaroni and cheese, ate some pre-packed sandwiches, and washed it all down with delicious Wyler's powdered juice drinks. Grape was my favorite. Under a dark sky filled with countless stars and a totally visible Milky Way, we told our usual scary ghost stories. Finally, after bouts of uncontrollable yawning and the spreading of the yawn throughout the group, we checked our sleeping bags for snakes before crawling in them for the night. I listened to the lonely calls of the coyotes. They seemed to come closer and closer to us. I just lay there listening to the night world and couldn't sleep. Then, something came over me in the middle of the night. It started as just an evil random thought as the coyotes continued their yelping and howling. Coyotes are the tricksters in Native American lore. Perhaps inspired by those animal tricksters, I decided to dislodge that giant boulder and roll it down the cliff. The drop would be several hundred feet to the Columbia River below. This random evil thought became a determined evil plan.

To make my devilish plan more interesting I thought that I should scream at the top of my lungs as the giant boulder began to rumble and tumble down to the river. As everyone was asleep, I quietly got out of my sleeping bag and put on my shoes. The stars provided enough light for me to conduct my trickster mischief. The coyotes were still howling and continued to encourage and dare me to carry out the deed. I found a sturdy stick and wedged it under the massive rock with a smaller stone and, with a fulcrum effect, attempted to move the boulder. It barely moved at first, but, undeterred, I gave it my all and finally the ancient rock came loose. Unfortunately, so did some of the ledge and I nearly fell over the rim myself. Or maybe I did fall? Could this have been another fork in the road of time? Had I fallen to my death as a result of my childish prank? Am I on another path now, another dimension where I lived through the ordeal? The boulder took a good chunk of the side of the ledge with it, much more than I thought, and it was loud. Extremely loud! I screamed bloody murder and gave it a doppler effect for authenticity. Everyone woke up immediately and sprang to their feet.

"What the fuck!?!"

"What was that?"

"Where's Bruce, did he fall off the cliff?!"

I couldn't contain myself and started laughing hysterically. My friends were not amused when they spotted me and realized it was a prank.

"We thought you were dead! You asshole!"

"What if someone was down below? You would have killed them!" I guess I didn't think of that.

"Unbelievable, Bruce, you're a real jerk. If someone was hurt or killed, I'm not covering for you!"

After a few minutes, they all went back to their sleeping bags muttering and grumbling and I stood there in silence, bewildered. What's the big deal? It was funny. A good practical joke. The coyotes had gone away and were no longer singing my praises. No backup. I eventually returned to my sleeping bag and drifted into a restless sleep. My dreams were strange and dark. Mysterious shadowy figures rising up from the cliffs were choking me. I barely slept that night.

The area around Vantage has been occupied by the Wanapum Indians since prehistoric times. The Wanapum inhabited the area from the Beverly Gap to the Snake River along the Columbia. They greeted Lewis and Clark when they arrived in 1805. The Wanapum never fought white settlers and never signed any treaties. Sadly, as a result, they have no federally recognized right to the land. Over 300 petroglyph rock carvings were discovered on the basalt cliff walls near Vantage on the Columbia River. They are more than 11,000 years old. Unfortunately, when the Wanapum Dam was built in the 1960s, the petroglyphs were flooded over except for 60 of them that were blasted out and preserved in the Gingko Petrified Forest State Park.

My pushing that boulder off of the cliff further disturbed the natural and sacred environment in the gorge. I didn't honor the Wanapum and their land. It was nature's sovereign decision for when that boulder was to fall, not mine. In other words, I certainly wasn't the "king of rock and roll." And neither was Elvis according to many music historians. When would I learn? Had I found yet another fork in the road of time in my life? I don't know for sure. A year later, lost, adrift, and having flunked out of the University of Washington, I joined the US Army to try to get control of myself and find some sort of direction. I know one thing for sure—I've learned not to listen to the coyotes.

FOLLOW ME (1977)

The Roslyn Cemetery, in Roslyn, Washington, has more than 5,000 graves. This tiny town on the east side of the Cascade Mountain range currently has a population of 893. The dead greatly outnumber the living in this historic city. Most of the early inhabitants were miners and railroad workers. Roslyn was founded when the Northern Pacific Railroad came through, and coal was discovered in 1886. The cemetery is made up of 25 different cemeteries bordering each other. These cemeteries are dedicated to various ethnic groups or fraternal lodges. Roslyn was an incredibly diverse town with more than two dozen nationalities represented in these cemeteries. In 1900, approximately 40 percent of the people were foreign-born, and 22 percent were African-Americans (initially brought in as strike-breakers). By 1963, the last working coal mine was shut down. Hippies and artists moved in during the 1960s and 1970s, and in the 1990s a TV show called *Northern Exposure* was filmed in Roslyn.

Being situated near Interstate 90, a major East-West freeway in Washington, I had passed by Roslyn for as long as I could remember. It wasn't until a Halloween night in 1977 that I visited the town. My girlfriend Marianne and I had been to Spokane to visit her friend and were on the way home to Seattle. We stopped in Cle Elum (a small town about four miles southeast of Roslyn) for dinner at the Cottage Cafe. Chicken-fried steak, yummy. I read about an old graveyard in Roslyn in the local paper that was lying on the table.

"I wanna go to the graveyard," I said.

"No," said Marianne.

"I'm serious," I said before Marianne cut me off.

"So am I," she snapped. I thought for a moment.

"It's Halloween, come on, let's have a spooky adventure, it's supposed to be haunted," I said.

"That's exactly why we're not going," she said. We sat in silence for a minute.

"We went to Spokane to visit your friend and I just wanna do this one thing," I said. She thought for a moment. It had not been an easy trip for me. Seeing her old boyfriend wasn't pleasant.

"Okay, but we're not staying long," she said. I celebrated internally.

By the time we got to Roslyn, it was dark and a little foggy. There was snow on the ground in patches and other than a few trick or treaters in town, no one else was around. When we reached the entrance to the cemeteries, the fog had lifted. I noticed a sign with cemetery rules: no dogs, no horses, no snowmobiles. That all made sense to me. Last rule: cemeteries closed after dark. What? I wondered why. Certainly we wouldn't be disturbing anyone. What were the city officials worried about? Graverobbers? Ghosts scaring people to death and having their surviving relatives sue the city? Weird.

Leaving our car behind, we proceeded on foot. I had a flashlight in my glove box and we took that with us. Nestled in among the tall pine trees and hillsides were the graves. We saw old tombstones covered in lichen and moss, weathered by decades of rain, snow, wind, and sun. Some of the plots had short iron fences surrounding the graves; others had broken down wooden fencing. Many of the graves were overgrown due to neglect and some of the headstones were toppled over, perhaps due to vandalism. Each cemetery section on the 25-acre site had its wooden sign. There was the Mt. Olivet Cemetery section where African-American miners were buried, the Independent Order of Odd Fellows (IOOF), the Knights of Pythias Lodge, and the Improved Order of Redmen, among many others.

We finally reached the Old City Cemetery. The sign read: The Old City Cemetery is the oldest cemetery in Roslyn, founded in 1886. The cemetery contains the remains of miners who died in the coal mines and young children who died from numerous epidemics here. There were lots of little kid graves. Very creepy. I started to feel the hair on the back of my neck and my arms, raise on end. Marianne wanted to leave.

"Someone will come and get us in trouble," said Marianne.

"Don't worry," I said.

"Listen, I don't wanna end up in some small-town jail," she added. I glanced at my girlfriend and smiled.

"Come on, there's nobody here, and nobody cares," I said. The sound of breaking branches startled us.

"Time to get the hell outta here," she said.

"Wait, it's probably just an animal." My girlfriend wasn't smiling.

"Or the undead," I added. She hit my arm as I laughed.

"Let's keep going," I said. The full moon had now peeked out from behind the night clouds providing us with some light. I read some of the gravestone inscriptions.

"Look, this lady died in 1891," I said, "and here's her husband, he died in 1873, on Halloween." I read the inscription:

May he rest in peace. Sweet Jesus, have mercy on him. We have loved him in life, let us not forget him in death.

"That's too creepy," said Marianne. Just as I finished reading that epitaph, we heard branches snapping again, then we saw some lights across the graveyard, moving.

"What the fuck is that?" asked Marianne.

"I don't know," I said.

"Let's just get out of here, now!" she said. We stood in silence for a few moments, no more sounds or lights.

"Just a little longer, I see an interesting gravestone over there," I said. The gravestone in question was covered in lichen and moss, and it was leaning against a fallen tree. Broken iron fencing lay on either side.

"Can't read the name," I said as I brushed away the pine needles. We were shocked to see what lay beneath the covering of pine needles, dirt, and sticks. The inscription read:

Where I lie, you shall soon be, so take my hand and follow me.

Above the epitaph was a carved hand reaching upward. A cold chill came over me and we stood frozen in our tracks. More branches were snapping, a few lights flickered across the graveyard, and we heard voices, muffled, but apparently human voices.

"That's all I can take, I'm outta here," said Marianne. She started for the car as I tried to hold her arm.

"Please stay," I said.

"Hell no! I'm crazy but not stupid," she answered quickly and took off. I was alone. I looked around, and all was quiet again. I walked to the car at a leisurely pace until I heard footsteps in the crunchy snow behind me. I stopped to look back, no one there. I picked up my pace and met her at the car.

"I told you this was a bad idea, now get in and let's go," said Marianne. My girlfriend was in the driver's seat of my Volvo station wagon. She peeled out of the parking lot in a hurry.

Recently, I read in the *Seattle Times* that ghost watchers had been denied permission to stake out the Roslyn Cemetery at night. The town council rejected the request by the Washington State Paranormal Investigations and Research (WSPIR) group. They wanted to investigate the reported eerie, odd, and unexplained phenomena at the cemetery.

"Let's not be the council that says OK to the ghost hunters," said one council member.

"This borders on hysteria," said another council member in support of the paranormal group, "I apologize to WSPIR. They're not going up there with picks and shovels." The council even banned the WSPIR from daytime visits and didn't allow them to post photos on their group website. The council chair said that having paranormal investigators at the cemetery "would be disrespectful to the dead and could result in the dislodging of fragile gravestones." The mayor of Roslyn was more enthusiastic and supportive of the request.

"I love it. Maybe they'll get up there and talk to my grandparents," she said.

Despite the ban by the city council, WSPIR members have visited the Roslyn Cemetery and have found evidence of paranormal activity near a mine shaft and even some electronic voice phenomena as well. Do you want to go and check it out? If so, follow me.

SOUTH NAKNEK (1978)

I'm not quite sure what lured me to Alaska, the land of the midnight sun. Perhaps it was my father and the stories he told me of his adventures as a fisherman; maybe it was the pay, or maybe it was because I was tired of living in my brother Alf's garage. On May 5, 1978, my plane took off from Seattle-Tacoma International Airport bound for Anchorage, Alaska. We had a three-hour layover in Anchorage. My old friends Johnny and Tommy had moved with their family to Anchorage a few years back, so I thought that I would look them up in the phone directory and call. Johnny and Tommy were not at home, but one of their sisters, Kallie, was. She told me that Tommy had lived in Anchorage for a while, but then he joined a religious cult and moved to California. Johnny was still in Alaska and was working up in Prudhoe Bay.

From Anchorage, we flew to King Salmon. The King Salmon airport was also home to a small Air Force station that was part of the North American Aerospace Defense Command (NORAD). The civilian part of the airport was a sight to see. All the buildings were made from corrugated aluminum. I spotted a snack bar and went in to wait for my flight out. In the snack bar, there were several patrons including four German tourists talking about big game hunting. On the walls hung huge animal head trophies. The Germans were about to take off for two weeks on a hunting trip with a seasoned Alaskan guide. King Salmon, I was to learn later, was a major point of embarkation for hunting and fishing tourism in Alaska. This kind of tourism was a major industry in the state.

The snack bar also served as a tavern, airline reservation office, and general provisions store. No building space went to waste in Alaska. One of the guys I was traveling with began to show interest in a drunk woman draped over the bar. He acted as if he had been up north for months instead of just a few hours. Luckily, before anything could happen, an airport worker came in and told us that our plane was ready. One of the bar patrons quaffed his beer and stood up.

"Time to saddle up boys," he said. So that was our pilot? He walked like he was drunk.

The bush pilot wore a beat-up leather flying jacket and a greasy red baseball cap. His whiskered and leathery face revealed a life of hard drinking and hard living. A patch on his jacket read "The Gunslingers," referring to a combat helicopter outfit he was probably with during the Vietnam War. I felt as if I were back in the Old West. The plane was a single-engine six-seater. We had five passengers plus all our tools and other baggage. Somehow, the pilot and his ground crewmen got all the gear on the plane. As we all piled in, the tail of the plane rocked back tilting the nose skyward.

"God damn it," the pilot said to the ground crew, "hold the tail up while I take off you fuckers." As ridiculous as it sounds, we taxied to the runway and began our takeoff assisted by the two ground crewmen holding the tail of the aircraft up and jogging beside us. Once we had built up enough speed, they were left in our dust, and we remained level. My life flashed before my eyes, and I began to think that this wasn't such a good idea. The old plane creaked and groaned down the runway and used every inch to take off. We reached an altitude of about ten feet and remained there for a few minutes. Straining under the weight, the old plane struggled higher into the sky and finally achieved a cruising altitude of 200 feet or so. It was then that the pilot suddenly yelled out:

"Shit, I forgot to top off the fuel in this fucker." I thought to myself that I was a dead man. Even if I did survive the crash, the grizzlies, those beastly bruins of the tundra, would feast on me. I accepted my fate, whatever it would be. Luckily, the flight from King Salmon to South Naknek wasn't that long, and the fuel held out.

The tundra beneath us was beautiful and unspoiled. There were no roads or telephone wires or anything to indicate civilization. I wondered if Washington State had looked like that at one time. After twenty minutes in the air, I spotted the mouth of a large river emptying into the ocean. We had arrived in Bristol Bay and the little town on the south side of the river was South Naknek. Using my keen insight, I figured the small town on the north side of the river was North Naknek, but I found out later that it was called just Naknek. We flew low over the abandoned fish cannery complex at South Naknek that was to be my home for the summer. Cutting the engines twice to signal our arrival, the pilot set up for his approach. The guy sitting next to the pilot asked if he had to contact the tower to land. We dove suddenly down towards the runway and started our landing.

"What tower?" the pilot said, "We just look around and if no one's coming, we land. Shit, it's fucking easy man." The pilot made a relatively smooth landing considering the rough gravel runway and we taxied to a parking lot filled with an unnerving collection of broken airplanes.

"What happened to those planes?" I asked.

"Bad landings," said our pilot.

A bearded man in a green hunting outfit met us as we popped out of the crowded aircraft. He was accompanied by a nice-looking, tomboyish woman with a cracked front tooth who smelled of men's cologne. So, this was South Naknek.

We drove in a pickup truck to our billeting. The old cannery building was built on pilings and hung partially over the water. I was told to pick a room upstairs in the building and found a room with a window that overlooked the ocean. Then I met our foreman, a tall, good-natured man named Fred.

"I'm the foreman until the others come," Fred said. He repeated this statement several times a day. I found out that we were to work twelve to fourteen hours a day. At first, that sounded ridiculous until I was told that we would have several coffee breaks or mug-ups as the Alaskans call them. Since South Naknek had only a post office, a grocery store, and a bar, and there wasn't anything else to do, the long working hours were not that bad. There were only six miles of road around South Naknek. In Alaska, these would be called roads, in the lower forty-eight, they would be considered trails at best. Only four-wheel drive trucks could drive on them. The native Aleut Indians used three-wheeled motorcycles to get around.

In the next few weeks, I learned that our primary mission in South Naknek was to assist the company's fishing fleet by maintaining the boats and supporting fishing operations. I was a general helper and carpenter. One of my fellow workers at the abandoned cannery was Dan, the craggy-faced welder. He told me that he had skipped parole back in Seattle.

"I was in for manslaughter. I killed the guy who was raping my sister," he told me. There was also Will, the mechanic, who was hidden behind his full, black beard and thick glasses. Will said that he changed his last name so often that he could not remember his real one. He advised me always to keep the same first name if I was ever to change identities. Then there was Lee, the friendly handyman who was trying to hire on to a fishing boat. He was of Norwegian heritage, like me, and had the requisite dark Nordic sense of humor. One day when he was helping Dan do some welding, a spark settled into his hair and began smoldering. He looked up at Dan and the shower of sparks cascading down on him.

"Fucking hair, god-damned hair," he said as he laughed and patted his balding head and smothered the smoldering embers.

Time seemed to stand still. Although I was making a lot of money, I was miserable. I could not really connect with any of the other workers. After working for a week and not leaving the cannery complex, I finally decided to explore a little. I walked up to the tundra plateau that overlooked the inlet and the bay. The sweeping tundra grassland waved rhythmically with the strong gusts of wind. Small wildflowers were beginning to appear, and the ground was spongy beneath my feet. It was a beautifully raw and chilly landscape where the temperature never got above 48 degrees or so for the whole time that I was there.

I decided to walk down along the inlet and explore the other abandoned canneries, some of which were entirely deserted not having been converted for other purposes like ours. The old canneries were a testimony to an earlier time when fortunes were being more easily made from Alaskan fish resources. With too much competition and reduced fish catches, the canneries began to shut down. The weathered gray boards of the old cannery walls were being peeled off by the howling arctic winds that blasted the sides of the buildings. I felt an intense loneliness there as I looked out across Bristol Bay to the Bering Sea. I was really in the last frontier; the real Wild West. I was on my own, no one to watch over me, so different from my sheltered life at home. Then I heard some hammering noises in a boat house down by the water. I decided to explore the origin of the noises later since I had to get back to my job.

The next day, I went back to the boat house where I heard the hammering sounds. I peeked inside and saw a man working on a timeworn wooden fishing boat.

"Howdy, my name is Bruce, how ya doing?" I said.

"Hi Bruce, I'm just fine, my name's Chris," he said with a gentle smile. He had a short-trimmed beard and wore a red flannel shirt with suspenders. Chris told me that he had bought an old wooden boat and was making it seaworthy for the salmon season. Chris was a kind, intelligent man and much easier to talk to than the ex-cons back at the cannery. He told me that it was good for me to be up in Alaska and learn something of the outside world and gain experience. I told him how much I hated my job at the cannery complex. Chris said that he had a friend coming up from Seattle to help him fish. Otherwise he would have let me work with him. After we had spoken for some time, he told me that he had been in the Vietnam War. Chris said that being up in Alaska helped him forget the painful memories he had of the war. I spoke to him a couple more times before I decided to leave Alaska.

"Always try to do good, even in a bad situation," he said, "set a good example, then perhaps others would follow."

The last days before I decided to leave, I headed into the village and met some of the Aleuts. I went to a community basketball game and got to play. I was like a giant to them. I was six feet, two inches, which was about six to eight inches taller than any of them. I had a great time, although their style of basketball was more like wrestling. At the game, I met an Aleut my age named Hank, and he introduced me to Mary, his sister who was the local school teacher and about six years older than me.

"Not too many of the whites up here want to have much to do with us," said Hank, after he invited me to a party they were having that night. The party was going to be on the bluff above the old cannery.

I got to the party just before it started to get dark. The Aleuts had a huge fire going. I sat down next to Hank and Mary and listened to some of the old stories the Aleuts were telling. Chris, the fisherman, was talking to some of the elders. I was mesmerized by the fire and probably had too many beers. Mary kept inching closer to me, and Hank disappeared. I was drinking beer, and the fire, the singing, and storytelling was starting to make me feel like I was in a dream. We stared at the fire and began moving in sync with the flames as they shot high up toward the stars. We laughed and understood. I began to feel like I was shooting up with the flames into the heavens as I held Mary's hand. It was a magical feeling, but then reality set in, I was leaving Alaska.

After a few hours, I decided to go back to my room and sleep. Mary said she would walk back with me. I wondered if that was a signal that we might have sex. We were walking on the trail down the bluff to the cannery when I lost my footing and fell. I fell down the embankment above the cannery. It seemed like I fell in slow motion. Luckily, I didn't hit any of the big rocks on the way down, and I tumbled safely to the sand at the bottom. I must have fallen about one hundred feet. I was stunned but came around as I stood and looked up at the steep embankment. There, on top of the bluff, stood Mary, Hank, and Chris. The glow of the fire and the moon silhouetted them against the dark, starry sky. They raised their hands as if to wave and then they were gone. How did I survive that fall? Was it because I had been drinking beer? Was it the work of my guardian angel again? Had I reached another fork in the road of time? Maybe I did die from that fall and immediately started another alternate life path. I don't know.

The next day, I told Fred, the foreman, that I was leaving. I could not work with those ex-cons anymore. I had to go home. On the flight back to Seattle, I began to think about my strange adventure in Alaska and wondered if I would ever go back there again. I felt as if I didn't complete what I started to learn up there. It was like I left part-way through a movie. I recently discovered that our Vice President of Instruction and our Dean of Language Arts at Citrus College where I teach have both worked in South Naknek. What are the chances of the three of us ending up at the same place?

AWOL (1979)

I joined the US Army on Halloween 1978 after arguing with my father. By March 1979, I had completed basic and advanced individual training and was ready for my deployment. When I first arrived at my unit—the 77th Military Police Detachment—in Mannheim, West Germany, it was on a Friday evening in the middle of March 1979. The CQ (a sergeant in charge of the quarters) assigned me to a second-floor room. The MP barracks were built during World War II and showed their age. In fact, most of the US Army buildings in Germany were from the Second World War. I dragged my duffel bag into the room and found three black soldiers who were surprised to see me.

"Hello," I said.

"Hey," said one of the soldiers. I remembered him, Jefferson, I went through basic training with him.

"Whatcha think you doing? No, no, you ain't staying here," said another soldier. The third soldier said nothing and just gave me a steely death stare. I found the empty bunk and put my gear in a metal locker. They were talking to each other in hushed tones, so I couldn't make out what they were saying.

"I'm a little tired," I said as I laid down on the uncomfortable army bed.

"Awright," said Jefferson. The others said nothing and just stared at me with contempt. I had no lock for my locker so, when I thought the guys weren't looking, I decided to put my money under my pillow as I slept. I didn't know at the time, but the barracks were segregated–not by the army or the commander, but by the soldiers themselves. I already sensed that my new roommates were not pleased with me. As I began to fall asleep, I could hear them talking.

"We gotta get rid of this Gomer Pyle mother-fucker," said the one who hadn't spoken to me.

"How we gonna do that?" asked the other guy.

"Ah, he's awright, he didn't do nothing," said Jefferson.

I woke up the next morning to find $200 in cash missing. Luckily the traveler's checks were still under my pillow. Apparently, someone had reached beneath my pillow in the middle of the night to steal my money. I also found a heavy steel bunk leg segment lying on the floor by the head of my bunk. Was the thief going to hit me in the head with that if I woke up? What the fuck! I made a quick decision. I was leaving. I had a civilian passport, unbeknownst to the Army so that I could travel throughout Europe without Army permission. I put on my civilian clothes and left for the Mannheim Bahnhoff (train station).

I was going to Norway. I figured I could stay with my Nazi aunt in Oslo for a while and then eventually make it up north to the island where my parents still had a homestead. The bahnhoff was crowded and I finally made it to the front of the line. In my Americanized German, I ordered a ticket. The ticket agent apparently misunderstood and printed a ticket for Osloß instead of Oslo. This situation was particularly distressing because Osloß was in East Germany. One could only imagine what would happen to a US soldier traveling in communist East Germany on a civilian passport. Luckily, a friendly German college student behind me in line stepped in to help.

"He needs a ticket to Oslo, Norway," he told the agent in German.

"Thank you," I said to the stranger. The thoroughly annoyed ticket agent tore up the ticket to East Germany and printed a ticket for Oslo instead.

"Have a nice trip," said the helpful stranger.

Everything went well on the train from Germany and through Denmark until I reached Sweden. I thought it was cool how the train went directly on to a ferry to make the passage across to Sweden, until I was awakened by a large female Swedish immigration officer.

"Passport!" she demanded. She had her leg between my legs and was most insistent that I produce some identification papers. I fumbled for my passport, and she snatched it from my hands.

"Ah, an American," she said. The only problem with my civilian passport was that the photo showed me with wavy shoulder-length hair. Now that I was a soldier, my hair was barely one-quarter of an inch long. She looked at the picture, then me, the picture, then me again. I felt that I was doomed.

"Is this you?" she asked.

"Yes, it's me," I answered.

"Hair very short now," she said.

"Ya, more comfortable," I said. She was going to figure out I was a US soldier and ask for my military travel papers; I just knew it. Instead, she gave the passport back to me and moved on. I sighed heavily knowing that I was more than lucky.

I arrived in Oslo in the evening and called Aunt Walborg, my Nazi aunt, from the station. She was surprised that I was visiting unannounced and suggested that I take a taxi to her house where she would pay the driver. It wasn't long after I arrived that my aunt became suspicious.

"Did you run away from the Army?" she asked. I broke down and told her the story. Her husband, my uncle Ragnar, looked on.

"This is what happens when you give black people anything. They run wild!" she said in Norwegian. I regretted mentioning that the soldiers were black.

"Jefferson didn't do it, I'm pretty sure, he's a good guy," I said.

"They're all the same, just like the Paki's here in Norway," she said referring to the recent influx of immigrants from Pakistan to Norway. She insisted that I call my father in America. My dad wasn't happy. I spent the weekend, maybe three days, in Oslo. Aunt Walborg consulted an attorney regarding asylum, and the prospects seemed grim because of Norway's NATO partnership with the United States. My aunt was nice to me, almost too nice. I suspected that I knew why, but I didn't have time to think of the past in the middle of that crisis. Dad called again.

"Go back to Germany, tell them what happened, maybe they'll go easy on you," my dad advised. Then my brother got on the phone.

"You're making things hard for Mom and Dad, go back and explain it, maybe you won't get too much punishment," he said. I felt ashamed. I knew what I had to do, and I accepted my fate. I thought how ironic it was that I came to Germany to work in a military prison, and now I was going to end up being a prisoner myself. The Army tended to frown on soldiers who leave their duty assignments without permission. I thanked Aunt Walborg and my uncle Ragnar and my aunt gave me my grandfather's old leather satchel when I left. They were both acting weird.

"Maybe it will bring you luck," she said. The train ride back to Germany went smoothly, and I was prepared to face the worst upon returning to my unit. I figured it wasn't a matter of if I would go to prison, but for how long I would be imprisoned. Much to my surprise, no one knew I was gone, and my duffel bag was still in my locker untouched. It was a miracle. The CQ had never bothered to enter me into the incoming log five days earlier, so I was never scheduled for in-processing. The clerk in the orderly room was bewildered and suspicious.

"Didn't I see you last week?" the orderly room clerk asked me as Jefferson popped into the office. I didn't answer. The clerk looked at me and then at Jefferson.

"Hasn't this guy been in your room, Jefferson?" the clerk asked. Jefferson looked at me then at the clerk.

"Nah, he just came in. All these white boys look alike ya know," he said with a grin. Everyone laughed. Later I thanked Jefferson and asked him about the money. He told me that the other two guys probably took my money after he stepped out.

"They're heroin addicts," he added. I was officially signed into the unit as if I had just arrived from the states. My guardian angel was protecting me again.

MY WAGNERIAN FORD (1980)

I bought a two-tone green German-made 1966 Ford Taunus from a German man behind the post exchange (PX) in Mannheim, West Germany, in October 1979. He said his name was Franz and he told us that he worked at one of the auto shops behind the PX. After I had bought the car and it broke down, I took it to the shop where he said that he worked and asked for Franz.

"He used to work here, but I fired him," the owner said. "He was a crook!" he added as my heart sunk.

Great, now I was stuck with a worthless piece of junk car, I thought. Every time I stopped, broken glass and hair curlers would pour out from under the dash. It did have a lovely paint job, though.

If that wasn't bad enough, we lived in an apartment above a noisy German gasthaus (which is like a bar with a few rooms to rent) at 52 Memeler Strasse in Mannheim. Every night we heard the jukebox playing loudly and people drinking and trying to talk over the music. Pink Floyd's "Just Another Brick in the Wall" played day and night. On Thursday nights, the old German war veterans would gather for their meeting wearing green uniforms. They would gobble down dozens of schnitzels, drink beer, and *schunkel* (join arms and sway to and fro) to old German songs. As the evening wore on, and after more beer and shots of Jägermeister, the songs they were singing started to sound like old Nazi songs from World War II. On other nights, occasionally a fight would break out down on the street in front of the gasthaus. It was usually the Moped Mommas. They were the German equivalent of a motorcycle gang. They drove mopeds instead of Harleys, that fact alone made them seem less threatening than their American counterparts. Between the stress caused by my dumb car, the lack of sleep from the gasthaus racket, and the rotating shifts at the prison, my health was deteriorating.

My car kept getting progressively worse. I'm pretty sure it was possessed and was trying to kill me. The steering would go out suddenly and the electrical system would fail, usually at night. At least twice a week it would not start, and I would have to get the battery charged by a local German garage. By January 1980, the garage mechanic would no longer charge my battery. He told me to buy a new car. The car was so bad that my friends who didn't own cars would rather take public transit than ask for a ride. One time, I was driving through a German neighborhood during the time of year when they all put old furniture out on the street. The Germans called it *junking*. I parked in a particularly narrow street that morning as I was looking for a desk. By the time I returned to my car, a garbage truck had appeared and wanted to get by me. My car's drive linkage didn't work very well, so I couldn't put it into reverse to back up and let the truck pass. I tried to explain this to the driver, but he thought I was being an asshole. I sat in my car gesturing for him to back up. Finally, he came over and reached in my car window and grabbed the shifter on the steering column. He jammed it down hard, and it broke loose and spun around the column like an imbalanced pinwheel. He looked at me with disgust and slapped his forehead.

"*Dummkopf*," he said in German, meaning blockhead. But instead of backing his truck up so I could drive by, he woke up a lady on the other side of the street and had her move her car. She came out in her bathrobe and curlers to comply.

Another time, my car stalled on the streetcar tracks just as the streetcar was approaching. German trains, buses, and streetcars run on time. Nothing will delay them. Even running over people or crushing cars aren't outside of the realm of possibility to keep a schedule. The streetcar was coming and was sounding its warning horn as I was trying desperately to push my car off the tracks. At the last moment, two other GIs saw my plight and helped me.

"Close call," one of them said. I nodded my head in agreement.

"I'm ready to get rid of it. Wanna buy a car?" I asked. They both looked at me and laughed.

"No, man. I got enough problems," said the other soldier.

I was convinced that my car was trying to kill me, but we were planning a trip to Austria, and we could not afford a new car. To get to Austria, we would have to use the autobahns, something I had avoided because autobahns require high-speed driving. I remembered, during orientation when I arrived in Germany, the sergeant told us not to try to cross the autobahn on foot.

"A few have tried, all have died," he said.

We all laughed.

"Shut up assholes. I'm not lying. If they hit you, and they will hit you, you'll be dead. There's no speed limit, and those fuckers drive very fast!" he said.

"And, your family will have to pay for damage to Herman German's car," he added. I was terrified to think of getting on the autobahn in my car, much less crossing the autobahn on foot.

In June 1980, I finally had had it with the dumb car. The final straw came when we took another trip to Austria. My friends had to hold flashlights out of the windows to simulate headlights because as soon as darkness came, we had an electrical failure. We could only go about 40 to 50 kilometers per hour and in only one gear. The standard speed on the autobahn was about 140 kilometers per hour. German cars sped by us like we were standing still. We somehow made it to Austria and back, but on the way back, the transmission linkage broke, and I couldn't disengage the clutch. We stalled out at every traffic light and had to start again every time by compression.

I tried to sell my car for parts, but nobody even wanted the parts. Finally, exasperated, I drove the car to the junkyard playing the radio at a high volume. It was a classical station, and they were playing a Richard Wagner piece. I stalled the old car in the middle of the junkyard and turned off the ignition. It continued to run and sputter, trying not to die. No matter, I was done, so I got out and removed my green US military plates. As I was walking away, I saw some of the guys who refused to buy the parts from my car descending on it like vultures.

What assholes, I thought. Then, finally, the engine backfired with a loud bang like a cannon shot. I was startled and turned around in time to see the old beast burst into flames. The backfire explosion and fire frightened away and scattered the parts vultures. I smiled as I walked away and the flames grew higher and brighter. My demon car was returning to Hell from where it came.

AT LEAST WE'RE NOT ZERO (1980)

When I was five or six years old, I began to have moments where I was suddenly fully aware of my consciousness. This feeling of intense awareness was startling to me and gave me quite a jolt every time it happened. It would usually begin with everything speeding up around me and then culminate in me looking in the mirror and saying, "Who is that?" Then, "Oh yeah, that's me! I'm a real person." As odd as that sounds, I would go through this startling realization of my consciousness a few times a year. So, what was I doing the rest of the year? Sleepwalking? I never tried to tell anyone because I thought it was normal, or if it wasn't normal maybe people would think I was weird. In high school, I would occasionally drift into a meditative state and not have sensation in my body temporarily. I also told no one about those experiences. I believe that I was slipping into alpha brainwave states and didn't know it. No wonder I'm a lightning rod for the paranormal. As remarkable as these phenomena were, my teenage self took it as a sign of weakness, and I felt weird and out of control, as it further damaged my self-esteem.

In 1980, while I was working at the US Army Confinement Facility in Mannheim, West Germany, I was having a life crisis. I was married and had one child and knew that I had a lot to learn. My temper always seemed to get the best of me and I didn't know why. I decided to go back to college. I had dropped out of the University of Washington in 1978 to join the Army. My first class was a drafting class through Big Bend Community College. I loved it.

The next class was Parapsychology. I had had many paranormal experiences up to that point and had always been fascinated by such things, so the course held great appeal to me. The course was taught by a clinical psychologist (I'll call him Dr. Randy) who specialized in autism and Dr. Christopher Mooney who held a Doctor of Divinity degree. Dr. Randy was a skeptic, and Dr. Mooney was a believer. That dichotomy provided for an interesting pedagogical dialectic for us as students. Our textbook was *Parapsychology: Its Relation to Physics,*

Biology, Psychology, and Psychiatry, edited by Gertrude R. Schmeidler. I couldn't get enough of the paranormal.

One day, after class, I approached Dr. Mooney to ask for his advice. My wife Anna and I fought a lot. I know that I was abusive to her and later in our marriage I would be arrested for this terrible mistreatment she endured. I wanted to talk to Dr. Mooney because earlier that day I had pushed my wife during an argument, and she had fallen and accidentally hit her head on the bathtub. I knew my anger was out of control, I was in trouble and needed help. As soon as I approached him and before I had uttered a word, Dr. Mooney looked at me and knew, as if he could read my mind.

"Go, take care of your wife, your family, and yourself, then come back to the next class, if you are ready," he said.

It was the beginning of my recovery and healing. He was a legitimate psychic. I loved the class and learned so much. As our final assignment, I wrote a research paper entitled, "Meditation: A Link to the Unknown." This paper has manifested itself as the walking meditation I do today.

Our Parapsychology class was held in the Coleman Barracks Education Center which was previously a Nazi administration building. Coleman Barracks was a former Nazi military base. We had a large classroom with high ceilings and tall windows. The building was filled with history and ghosts. One day, Dr. Mooney and Dr. Randy, the skeptic psychologist, were debating fiercely about the legitimacy of miraculous stories in the Bible.

"So, for instance, you would have us believe that the biblical story of the archangel Gabriel blowing his horn was real and that is what made the walls tumble down?" asked Dr. Randy.

"It was a trumpet, for God's sake, and we're not sure that it was the archangel Gabriel who blew the trumpet, and…" said Dr. Mooney.

"Who cares?" said Dr. Randy.

"Also, perhaps you're confusing the story of Joshua and Jericho with the archangel Gabriel and the rapture,"

Dr. Mooney went on to explain that in the Book of Joshua (6:1-5), Joshua was told by God to encircle and march around the City of Jericho (now situated in the Palestinian Territories, near the Jordan River, in the West Bank) for six days. On the seventh day, seven priests with seven trumpets were to march with the army around the city seven times and the people were asked to shout in unison with the trumpets. When this was done, the walls of Jericho trembled and collapsed.

"Okay, so, where does the archangel Gabriel come in?" asked Dr. Randy.

Dr. Mooney explained that it's popular in Christian lore to say that the archangel Gabriel blows his trumpet to announce Judgment Day or the Rapture or the end of the world, thereby associating the divine, or infinite, with the finite. Dr. Mooney turned to a chapter in his Bible.

"To quote the New Testament, 1 Thessalonians 4:15-17. 'For this we say unto you by the word of the Lord, that we which are alive [and] remain unto the coming of the Lord shall not prevent them which are asleep. For the Lord himself shall descend from heaven with a shout, with the voice of the archangel, and with the trump of God: and the dead in Christ shall rise first: Then we which are alive [and] remain shall be caught up together with them in the clouds, to meet the Lord in the air: and so shall we ever be with the Lord.'"

Dr. Randy was patient, but not impressed as Dr. Mooney continued reading.

"And from 1 Corinthians, 15:51-52. 'Behold, I shew you a mystery; We shall not all sleep, but we shall all be changed, In a moment, in the twinkling of an eye, at the last trump: for the trumpet shall sound, and the dead shall be raised incorruptible, and we shall be changed.'"

We were all impressed with this biblical knowledge, except for Dr. Randy.

"These are the only passages in the Bible that refer to a final trumpet. The first one doesn't refer to a trumpet but a voice like a trumpet. Neither one mentions the archangel Gabriel, although John Milton's epic poem *Paradise Lost* (1667) does identify Gabriel as the trumpeter," said Dr. Mooney. Dr. Randy stared blankly, unimpressed, unmoved.

"The Bible is filled with mystery and the paranormal. If God isn't paranormal, who is?" said Dr. Mooney. The room was anticipating a rebuttal from Dr. Randy, and after ten seconds it came.

"Nonsense," said Dr. Randy. We could tell that Dr. Randy, the ever-skeptical scientist, was incredulous and a bit embarrassed by Dr. Mooney.

"I've never claimed to be a biblical scholar. I'm a scientist. Besides, it makes no difference. Walls, rapture, horns, trumpets, saxophones, God, angels, whatever! It's all ridiculous made-up fictional superstition anyway!" he said.

We were all silent for a few moments. Then, one of the tall windows slammed shut with a jarring sound that nearly broke the glass scaring all of us, even the instructors. Then, before our hearts stopped racing from the first startling noise, another window slammed shut. We all stared at the windows, each other, and finally at Dr. Mooney and Dr. Randy. They began to laugh which caused all of us to laugh.

"That is what we get for your blasphemy," said Dr. Mooney as he continued to laugh.

Oddly, there is something called Gabriel's horn, it's a geometric figure that has infinite surface area but finite volume. Its properties were first studied by Evangelista Torricelli, an 17th century Italian mathematician and physicist. I survived the Army and continued my interest on and off with the paranormal. I continued to struggle with my self-esteem, I think this is partly to do with my upbringing, or at least my interpretation of my Norwegian half.

Norwegians, and all Scandinavians for that matter, tend to be rather modest. This regional cultural value stems from something called "Janteloven," which translated into English means, "the Law of Jante." The premise of Janteloven is that you're not to think you're anything special or try to hold your head up above anyone else. Jantelov was created in 1933 by a Danish-Norwegian writer named Aksel Sandemose. It was featured in his book entitled: *En Flytning Krysser Sitt Spor* (A fugitive crosses his tracks). Sandemose wrote about working-class people in the fictional Danish town of Jante. All the people in Jante held the same social position. This cultural attribute of humility was already common in Scandinavia for centuries, but never expressed the way Sandemose described in his book. Janteloven could also be used to justify criticizing people who are trying to climb up the socio-economic ladder. Americans pride themselves on their rugged individualism. We're competitive with one another. Scandinavians feel little of that pressure to keep up with the Jones, as we say in the United States. Janteloven calls for people not to compare yourself to others, instead, you compare yourself to yourself. Since Scandinavians are always rated as the world's happiest people, maybe there is something essential for us to learn about Janteloven.

One of my favorite movies from my childhood, from the Saturday scary movie selection on local TV, was *The Incredible Shrinking Man*. Made in 1957, a year before I was born. The main character, Scot Carey played by Grant Williams, is sprayed by a strange radioactive mist. He begins to shrink. The shrinking process is exacerbated by exposure to an insecticide. His marriage starts to fall apart. He meets a midget lady from a traveling circus who tells him being small isn't all that bad. He continues to shrink, and his wife assumes he is dead. He finally decides that no matter how small he becomes, he'll still matter in the universe, because to God, there is no zero. He loses his fear of what will happen as he continues to shrink to atomic size and smaller. For Americans, who always want to be the biggest, strongest, tallest, richest, and most popular, the thought of shrinking away to insignificant size is terrifying. Scandinavians, however, who have been inculcated by the spirit of Janteloven, would not think shrinking was all that scary. Norwegians, in fact, often call their country, "Little Norway."

The *Incredible Shrinking Man* film intrigued me then, and still does so today. I've come to think that the universe is both infinitely large and infinitely small. My continuing studies of the paranormal that formally began with Dr. Mooney and Dr. Randy in the parapsychology class in West Germany, have brought me to where I am today and led me to studies in quantum mechanics. I now know that my sudden feeling of self-realization is part of my special paranormal gift. I feel connected to the infinite, the spiritual realm. I'm convinced that the spiritual or paranormal realm is the quantum realm. I've come to grips with my place in the multiverse and let go of the anger, fear, and self-doubt that had driven my life for so long. Just how significant are we in comparison to infinite universes? Maybe we're not that big of a deal after all, but at least we're not zero.

HAUNTED HOUSE (1982)

I started to have recurring haunted house dreams in the 1980s and especially in 1989 after I found out that we would move to Ohio so that I could go to graduate school. My relationship with Anna wasn't going well and she didn't want to leave Washington State. I had a steady job working at Boeing as a buyer, and we had bought a house in Everett. She didn't want to uproot the boys and travel more than half-way across the country so that I could get my doctorate in history. She didn't see sense in making such a move. I had applied for a doctoral program at the University of Washington but was turned down. This rejection prompted me to apply at many different schools. Bowling Green State University in Ohio offered me a full-ride scholarship plus a graduate assistantship that paid $1000 per month. We set off across the country in December of 1989. I remember driving through North Dakota and the temperature dipping down to 30 below zero. I think the boys saw this as an adventure, but Anna didn't appreciate the hardships I was putting them all through. I understand now, but I didn't then.

The house in my nightmare is always the same. It's three stories high, old, falling apart, raised up from the street and on a hill, grey and weathered, and located, I believe, in Everett, Washington. Over the years, I've tried to figure out if this was a house that we've lived in or seen before. I've concluded that this haunted house of my dreams isn't a house that I've owned or lived in or have ever seen before in real life. I was born and grew up in Kenmore, Washington. I did own a house in Everett; it was an old home, built in 1921, but it isn't the house in my recurring dream. There was a scary house just north of our Everett home covered in blackberry bushes. We never saw anyone go in or out, but at night we could see a faint light in the window. I used to tell the boys that it was haunted to keep them away from it. But my nightmare haunted house is three stories tall, and the scary house covered in blackberry sticker bushes was one story with a daylight basement.

The nightmare haunted house is more like a house I rented in Tacoma, Washington, in 1996. That house, located on North 21st Street near the University of Puget Sound, was three stories tall, and definitely spooky. It was set up on a little hill above the street and surrounded by scary old trees that scratched against the house when it was windy. Since that old house wasn't insulated, the wind would find its way through the cracks and old unsealed windows inside making eerie whistling noises. In that Tacoma house, I did see the ghost of a middle-aged woman in stretch pants walking in and out of the laundry room. I think she died in the home; maybe a suicide. It was a neglected rental house filled with rats in the walls and hidden spaces. I felt particularly maniacal in that house with extreme outbursts of anger like I hadn't seen before. Caitlin was born while we lived in that house.

But even that Tacoma house from 1996 wasn't the house in my nightmares. The nightmare house is dilapidated and has a screened in back porch that enters a kitchen with an old wood burning stove and 19th century fixtures. The haunted house is situated on a steep hill road, and the house sits up from the road. The three stories contain empty rooms or rooms with old dusty dark furniture and felt as if we were moving out or just moving in. There are also small hidden rooms within rooms and hidden spaces between the walls. The house is lit by kerosene lantern or candles and has a weird cold feeling and is filled with evil spirits. The house seems familiar, like it's mine, but it isn't. The weather in my nightmare is always grey and dark, and the floors are a little crooked as well.

Dream experts say that haunted house dreams are complex and not as easy to interpret as other dreams. They say that the recurring dream is symbolic of unfinished emotional business related to childhood, dead relatives, or repressed memories and feelings. It could also have something to do with the dreamer's surroundings or sleeping environment. Experts also say that haunted house dreams indicate that the dreamer needs to grow spiritually. But, then again, who doesn't need to grow spiritually? Apparently, haunted house dreams aren't common. It may suggest that the dreamer is stuck in the past and needs to resolve those issues so that they can move on with their life.

Dream analysts also feel that the details of the haunted house suggest specific interpretations. They think that a tidy house is positive, a messy or dirty one is more negative. The familiarity of the house is significant. If you have seen the house from your dreams in real life, then that is positive. In my case, I've not lived in the house in my dream, and it's a mostly unfamiliar house. They also say that the part of the house you dream of is essential. I've dreamed of all parts of the haunted house.

Recurrent dreams occur in approximately 60 percent of adults, with more women dreamers than men. Psychologists and psychiatrists believe that recurrent dreams tend to fall into one of two categories: stress related or full-on nightmares. These dreams are associated with anxiety and fear: dreams of being chased, dreams of falling, and dreams of being in a haunted house. Dreams of falling may indicate transitioning from one sleep state to another. They believe that dreams of being chased where you can't move or are in slow motion are happening because you're in REM (rapid eye movement) sleep and your body is paralyzed. Some psychologists think that once the dreamer understands the message from the recurrent dream and makes appropriate positive changes, often the nightmares stop.

President Abraham Lincoln had a recurring dream that some significant event would happen very soon. His recurrent dream would happen just before an important event from the Civil War occurred. Lincoln had a cabinet meeting the afternoon before his assassination and told General Grant of his recurring dream and that something of great significance would happen soon. That evening he was shot by John Wilkes Booth and died the next day.

I've racked my brain to try to figure out where this familiar, yet not familiar haunted house exists. The answer finally came to me while I was running. It does exist, but as a composite of all the places I've lived. I figure that I've lived in more than 50 locations in my life. I know, I've moved a lot. The haunted house of my recurring dream is every house and place I've ever lived or maybe will live in, and none of them, not exactly anyway. As a composite, the haunted house of my dreams has just a piece from each place I've lived. Those homes and apartments have witnessed the positive and negative events in my life (and certainly from previous occupants as well) and those events have been collected and captured in those locations in my memory and have been dragged with me from place to place, layer upon layer. The ghosts follow me. It's my belief that once I complete the mission of excising those negative ghostly remnants, I'll stop having the recurring haunted house dreams.

ANGEL DUST (1982)

I was living with my family on a farm in Montrose, Minnesota, in the Summer of 1982. I was in the process of applying for flight school and was working on the farm and doing other odd jobs here and there. It was a waiting process until the US Army accepted me. I loved living on the farm, but it wasn't easy. There was always something to do, and it was always hard work. The uncertainty of whether or not the army would accept me was impacting my self-esteem. It didn't help that the only job I could find was a minimum wage position making pizzas at a local pizza joint. I couldn't go on living like that. What if the Army rejected my application? What would I do? How would I take care of my wife and two young children?

After a long shift at the pizza parlor, my brother-in-law picked me up and gave me a ride back home to the farm. We parked by the barn and he quickly reached into a box below his driver's seat. Inside the box was an assortment of pills, marijuana, and a piece of tin foil wrapped around something in a rectangular shape. He nodded to me and offered some of the drugs. I had smoked marijuana before, but not since high school. As we sat in his old bullet back Buick Riviera listening to "Black Magic Woman" by Santana on the radio, the sun was going down fast. Out of curiosity, I picked up the tinfoil rectangle.

"Want some?" he asked. I opened the foil and found a dark sticky substance.

"It's hash," he said.

"Hashish?" I asked. He smiled and nodded his head.

He grabbed a tiny pipe from the box and put a little chunk of the hashish in the bowl. He lit the pipe, took a toke, then handed it to me. I was reluctant. After almost a minute, I pushed the little pipe up to my lips, but then I exhaled and blew the tiny chunk of hashish out of the pipe. It landed on the dashboard.

"Hey, man, don't volcano it!" he said as he put the little piece back in the bowl and re-lit the pipe. My reluctance returned.

"I don't know," I said.

"Come on, it's good for you," he said.

I hesitated, but finally, I gave in. I noticed that the hash was very dark and had some white streaks in the sticky mixture. I took two drags and instantly felt strange.

"What is this stuff?" I asked.

"It's hash, man, I told you," he said. The strange feeling was spreading throughout my body quickly. I stared at the darkening sky and spotted the moon. It looked so big, almost like it was too big. Was it getting bigger? Weird thoughts like that came to mind.

"Isn't hash just a derivative of marijuana?" I asked.

"Yeah, don't ask so many questions, just enjoy the high," he said.

My mind raced as I began to lose sensation in my body and the stars came out and looked exceptionally bright, almost blinding me.

"I've smoked marijuana before, and I never felt like this," I said. He laughed at me.

"Just go with it," he said. I looked at the hash left in the tinfoil.

"What are those white streaks in the hash?" I asked.

"What?"

"The white streaks, right there," I said, pointing.

"Probably PCP, man, PCP, I think," he said.

My heart started pounding. I had heard of PCP, but it didn't immediately register.

"PCP—is there another name for it, like a street name or something?"

"Angel dust," he said.

I instantly began to panic.

"Angel dust!" I said. Angel dust wasn't anything I wanted to ingest. I had read stories about people on angel dust losing their minds and becoming like zombies. Supposedly cops fear people on angel dust because they can't feel pain and are entirely out of their minds. It was used as a horse tranquilizer in the past.

"You're fucking kidding me, right?"

"No, man, ain't it trippy?" he said. I was starting to freak out.

"Why didn't you tell me that there was angel dust in this?"

"You didn't ask," he said.

"Oh, shit!" I said as I felt the drug take hold of my mind and body. I knew I was in big trouble.

Phencyclidine (PCP), also known as angel dust, is a dissociative hallucinogen initially developed in the 1950s as an anesthetic and was used to tranquilize horses. The drug produces a trance-like state and can lead to out-of-body sensations. It's now illegal because it's considered too dangerous with too many side-effects. PCP can continue to affect a person for 4–6 hours depending on how much was ingested. It's often added to other drugs, such as marijuana or hash, as an extra booster. The effects can be felt in as little as one minute if smoked. Sights and sounds are distorted, a person can feel detached from their body and environment, and they can also have feelings of invincibility, super strength, and boundless power.

It was at this point that I decided to get out of the car and away from this crazy dude who continued to toke up the rest of the angel dust-streaked hash.

"Hey, where you going? There's more," he said.

I didn't answer as I tried to make my way into the old farmhouse slowly. After I took a few steps, I felt my body separate. There were now two of me. One was on the ground, and the other was floating just above.

"I'm so fucked up," I said. My brother-in-law was following me.

"You're fucked up, man," he said. "You're walking in slow motion."

It was all I could do to take each step. I had lost all sense of time and feeling in my body, or bodies. It seemed to take forever to get to the front door of the farmhouse. My brother-in-law was laughing at my expense.

"I think you got a major hit of the dust, man," he said.

"Thanks a lot," I said as I struggled to walk. I was both the grounded body and the floating body, but my floating body was in charge, so I thought.

I was praying that somehow, I could get to the basement where we were staying without anyone seeing me. No such luck. My mother- and father-in-law were in the living room watching *Wheel of Fortune*. They were old-world immigrants and would not understand me having an accidental bad trip on drugs. I would have to cross the living room in front of them to reach the stairs to the basement. My efforts to remain calm and not cause a distraction were making matters worse. I saw my in-laws sitting on the couch watching the game show and occasionally, staring at me. I looked at the screen, and the bright lights and colors mesmerized me. I might have stared at the screen for a few minutes instead of what I thought were a few seconds. My movements were slow and methodical, I thought, but this looked strange to my in-laws.

"Are you okay, Bruce?" asked my mother-in-law.

"Sure, hello, hi, how are you?" I said. I was waving to them as I walked in front of the TV screen. I could not determine time at this point. The angel dust was taking full effect. It probably took 20 minutes to get across that living room. With each slow step, I waved to them again. The lights and colors and noise from that stupid game show were freaking me out even more. Why did they have to be watching that show? I was smiling awkwardly and continued waving as I plodded across the room trying to maintain control of my grounded and floating bodies. I was providing as much entertainment as the TV at that point. To their credit, they continued to eat their dinners on their TV trays, unphased by my insanity.

Finally, I reached the stairs and, being thoroughly exhausted; I just let go of trying to control anything. It was just too complicated. I floated down the stairs not feeling anything. I continued to drift to my bed and laid down—at least my grounded body laid down. My floating body hovered above the bed, seeing all, feeling nothing. My brother-in-law had followed me.

"You are so fucked up, man," he said.

"Yeah, and it's your fault," I said.

"Hey, I didn't have a gun to your head," he said.

I was struggling to stay on the bed. It seemed as though even my grounded body was now floating along with my spirit body. Then I started spinning, just like Linda Blair in the Exorcist. I was spinning above the bed, both of my bodies. I was getting nauseous and was about to throw up. I needed some way to get my bodies together again and stop spinning. I was desperate. If I freaked out any more, someone would have to call 911.

"Hey, come over here and sit on me," I said to my brother-in-law.

"What?"

"Sit on me, so my bodies come together…I'm freaking out!" I said.

My brother-in-law sat on my back as I lay face down on the bed. It helped, a little.

"I swear, I'll never take any drugs for the rest of my life," I said.

My brother-in-law laughed as he lit a cigarette. "Whatever, man," he said.

I started praying. "God, get me through this, and I'll never use drugs again, I promise," I said.

My brother-in-law laughed again. The sensation of spinning slowed down, but I still felt like I was going to float away unless I had pressure on my back. Finally, I fell asleep. When I woke up the next morning, I had a terrible pulsing headache. My wife was in bed beside me.

"I heard you had quite a night," she said.

"Never again," I said.

"Okay, we'll see," she said.

I wonder how many people have accidentally taken angel dust? Probably not many, I would imagine. It was a terrible experience, and I learned a lifelong lesson from making this mistake. I should have known better. However, that being said, I now know what an out-of-body experience feels like from a first-person perspective. Although my out-of-body experience was drug-induced, it was exactly what other people have reported and felt in their near-death experiences. The PCP allowed me to glimpse the real nature of our existence. What I've determined is that we've both a physical and a spiritual body. The spiritual body isn't bounded by the same physical laws that constrain our physical body. That is probably what my friend Gene meant when he said that he doesn't need shoes.

"We just float," Gene told me. And that is precisely what I did. I would not recommend anyone taking PCP to achieve this effect and glimpse this rarely seen part of our existence. Let it happen naturally. Someday, we'll all get our angel wings and will no longer need to be tethered to our earthly bodies. Have no fear, dear readers.

THE STRANGER INSIDE (1983)

Carl G. Jung wrote: "Who looks outside dreams; who looks inside awakes." I've had recurring nightmares and visions throughout my life. These nightmarish dreams include haunted houses, tornadoes, tsunamis, explosions, volcanoes, and home invasion. It's fascinating and probably not coincidental that these recurrent nightmares represent air, fire, earth, and water—the four elements. There is a correlation between the four elements and Carl Jung's four psychological types or functions.

Air relates to thinking, fire to intuition, water to feeling, and earth to sensation. I believe that for me to heal myself psychologically and achieve tranquility in life, I need to balance these four essential elements within myself.

Air

My recurring tornado nightmares represent the air element. All my adult life I've had recurring tornado dreams. I believe these dreams stem from being traumatized when I was a pre-teen. I've experienced an actual tornado a few times, in North Carolina and Ohio, but I had tornado dreams before I lived in those states. The nightmare usually begins the same way; I'm at home in Seattle where I grew up. Our house sat at the top of a hill overlooking the Cascade Mountains and Mt. Rainier in the distance. I'm home alone, and suddenly the sky turns black and purple, and dozens of tornadoes form in the dark clouds. They're winding their way up from Lake Washington. As the twisters come closer and closer, the wind picks up and begins to howl, and the big trees outside are bending, and some of their branches are breaking. I continue to stare out the huge picture windows in our living room, frozen in fear. The air pressure drops dramatically as the winds pick up and the tornadoes approach, and I can see houses and cars and trees being sucked up into the vortex of each twister. The windows are straining and almost breaking under the pressure of the strong wind. I can't move. The sound is deafening. Then I wake up.

Therapists and dream experts say that tornadoes symbolize, extreme stress, significant changes, disagreements, and complicated relationships. That may be true, but that doesn't make the nightmares any less frightening or disturbing. My theory is that because we're elemental creatures, the elements must be in balance within us. I believe our dreams point out which element is out of balance.

Fire

My recurring fire dreams are associated with my time in the military. Some of these nightmares would place me at the site of a volcanic eruption. Intense heat, fire, molten rock, and ash raining down. I would run to get away just a few steps ahead of the fearsome lava flow and destruction. When I decided to enter flight school in 1983, I began having a new fire dream. I wrote about this in the story "Kill Tanks!" in my first *Timeless* book. In my nightmare, I'm flying in a helicopter by myself. Then, with a blinding flash and a fiery explosion, a missile or rocket destroys the aircraft, and I'm left by myself flying without the helicopter. I always wake up before I hit the ground.

Therapists and dream experts say that fire and volcano dreams symbolize that you are facing a major crisis in your life, have lost something, are challenging your fears through heroic action, are losing your temper, and are undergoing considerable upheaval in your life. While I was in the US Army, my family and I suffered through all those things. A personal crisis brought me into the Army, and I lost my first girlfriend because of my enlistment. I faced most of my fears and tested my courage many times in the military, whether it was working as a guard at the prison or flying. As part of the 82nd Airborne Division in the 1980s, we were continually standing at the precipice of war staring into the abyss. As a result, my life was in constant upheaval and made worse by my extreme anger outbursts including throwing and breaking furniture. Something had to change.

Earth

My home invasion and haunted house nightmares represented the earth element. The home invasion dreams were all the same. I'm sitting on a hill overlooking my house, and it's growing dark. My wife and children are inside our home. Then, a terrifying shadowy figure approaches the side door and begins to test the lock. He checks other doors and windows as well. He is trying to force entry into my house, as I sit there unable to move or even call out. It's as if my legs were broken or paralyzed and I'm mute. I can't help my family. He breaks in, and it's at this point that I wake up and the nightmare is over. After three failed marriages, violent temper outbursts, years of upheaval and chaos, and many years of personal therapy, I finally realized that I was the stranger and that I posed the greatest threat to my family and friends. I had to get well so that my family and I would be safe. Dreams have meaning, and the messages and warnings they deliver should be heeded. That was the Earth element. I needed to be safely grounded in my family and with myself.

Water

My father was a sailor, and all my ancestors in Northern Norway lived and died by the ocean. Norwegians are a seafaring people. Salt water is in my blood, and I feel most at home when I can see the mountains and the sea, as my mother used to say. My recurring water dreams involve tsunamis and crashing waves. As I sit in my house by the seashore, the tide rises suddenly. I watch through a large picture window as the sky grows dark and stormy and the waves begin to crash into the house. Each succeeding set of waves gets taller and more violent as it breaks. The water line is rising above me, and finally, a wave shatters the window, and water surrounds me. In a moment, I'm underwater, cold, swirling green sea water.

In my most recent tidal wave dream, I'm at a cliffside beach when I notice that the waves are growing larger. I begin to climb up the steep stairs to reach higher ground. On the way up, I see a plaque that commemorates the highest point that a wave had reached. I signal to my Citrus College friends on the beach and tell them to climb up. They tell me to come back down and stop trying to frighten people. I don't listen to them. At the higher level, I find a picnic table and sit down. At the table is my old friend Craig Higashiyama. Craig was a Vietnam War veteran and died several years ago of Agent Orange related cancer.

"The waves are getting higher and more violent," I tell him.

"They will get even bigger," he says.

"My Citrus friends told me that I'm wrong and should climb back down," I say.

"They're idiots," says Craig. The beach was familiar yet not familiar. Each wave grew larger and eventually came up and over us high on the cliff. There was no safe place in other words, no matter how high I climbed. The experts tell us that tidal wave or tsunami dreams symbolize illness or fear of disease, your worst fears coming true, turbulent emotions, a feeling of being overwhelmed, excessive worry about being loved, and a lack of confidence or self-esteem.

I believe that since my heritage is so closely tied to the sea, my life takes on the characteristics of the ocean. Sometimes I'm calm and in sync with the rise and fall of life each day, like the tides, and sometimes I'm raging like violent stormy breakers. They say that the strongest currents run deep. I do tend to bury my emotions, and those feelings can be overwhelming sometimes. For much of my life, I lacked confidence, and this lack of self-esteem would sour my relationships with loved ones. I've learned that you must love yourself and be proud of yourself. We must all be the hero of our own life story.

Having thought deeply about these recurrent dreams, I came to remember the first time I was left alone at home. It may have been when I was 11 or 12 years old. I still remember how terrified I was. I looked out of our big picture window down at 55th Avenue Northeast to see if I could see my parents driving home. Every creak in the house sent me into a panic. The cats knocked over a pan into the sink and the clanking and crashing noise nearly caused me to pass out. I cried and stared out the window for what seemed to be an eternity. That experience is probably why some of my recurring dreams have large picture windows featured prominently.

Sigmund Freud, the father of psychoanalysis, and Carl Jung, his former student, agreed that there was such a thing as the subconscious or as it later became known, the unconscious. They differed in what they believed its purpose to be. Freud believed the subconscious was a negative force of repressed immoral impulses. Jung, on the other hand, believed that it was a gift of wisdom and that dreams were a means by which the unconscious could communicate with the dreamer. Jung believed that every image seen in the dream reflected something within the person dreaming. Jung also believed that a trained professional along with the dreamer could decode dreams and determine their meaning tied to the symbolism unique to the dreamer. He went further with his theory of collective unconscious where all human beings shared a collection of symbols within their unconscious, across generations and cultures.

At this point in my life, at age 59, I'm getting closer to being balanced. The four elements are coming closer to balance with one another, and my life is more stable. I've had the same job for 20 years. I'm in my fourth marriage, but I've never been happier or more secure, and I've lived in the same area for nearly 20 years. All of that has given me the base from which to work on balancing the elements that we are all made of.

It's not surprising that this period of relative calm, especially the last ten years, has led to creative production as I've never known. I'm finally becoming the man I've always wanted to be and was supposed to be. I feel for all those who suffer from an imbalance in their lives. It leads to physical and emotional isolation. We stand guard against enemies, both perceived and real, because the world is filled with danger. Despite this threat, we must let others into our lives to live and enjoy life and prosper. I understand depression and I understand that the watch from inside of one's mind is the loneliest vigil of all. The stranger inside probably resides in what Freud and Jung called the unconscious. But, he isn't really a stranger, because the stranger is me, and we must become friends.

PRE-FLIGHT (1983)

I was listening to an audio book version of *The Gulag Archipelago* by Aleksandr Solzhenitsyn in early 2017, and it brought back a memory of mine. A painful one. While I was in the US Army Warrant Officer Flight Training (WOFT) program at Ft. Rucker, AL, from 1983 to 1984, we had to maintain immaculate wall lockers. This was especially true in the first phase of our training—WOC-D or Warrant Officer Candidate Development. It was very difficult for me to be that perfect. Every morning, the Training, Advising, and Counseling (TAC) officer would wake us up abruptly with clanging trashcans or by just screaming at us. We had five minutes to shit, shower, and shave. The TAC officer would then take us on a long run (usually five miles). When we returned from the run, we had to clean the barracks and our personal area consisting of a bunk and a wall locker. I remember having to unscrew the shower drains so we could spit shine them. I had a razor blade in my pocket that I shaved with on occasion to save me the time of having to clean my razor in the morning when they didn't give us enough time to do everything.

One day, Mr. Campbell the TAC officer, searched my pockets and found the razor blade. He told me that I was cheating the program, cheating the other candidates in my flight, and cheating myself and would be thrown out of flight school. I knew what that meant—the Army would throw me into the infantry and I would not get my wings and become a warrant officer. I was beyond devastated and filled with despair. They asked me to confess, but I refused. They told me that I had to sign the statement admitting that I had cheated. No way. I had shaved with that razor a few times, but not every time, only when the need arose. I wasn't the only one, believe me. Since I didn't confess, Mr. Campbell had me pulled out of the cycle and restricted me to barracks with the snowbirds who had not yet started WOC-D, the very beginning of flight training.

For one whole week, eight hours a day, I had to stand at attention outside of Mr. Campbell's office. Once per hour I was allowed to sit in a wooden chair for five minutes, then back to attention. My knees ached, my back hurt, and I was shaking, and sweating, because it was hot and humid in Alabama with no air conditioning. At lunch time they brought me food, I had ten minutes to eat sitting in my wooden chair. I wasn't allowed to talk to anyone except for the TAC officers. Every time Mr. Campbell passed by, he asked me to confess and sign the statement and I refused, respectfully. He would stand and look at me as he drank a cool glass of water, smiling.

"Just give up, admit it," he would say. "I'll make sure you get into cook school instead of the infantry, don't worry." Still I held out, no confession. After that week, they recycled me to the first week of WOC-D, and I would have to start all over again, several weeks behind my friends. Mr. Campbell was furious, but I could tell that some of the other officers were impressed with my tenacity and strength of will. It wasn't me though, it was my guardian angel. In my darkest hours at flight school when I didn't think I would make it, she was there. She helped me endure eight hours a day of standing at attention, and she got me through at the end of flight school when I failed my night vision goggle check ride and was recycled back another week and not allowed to graduate with my friends and take part in the fly-by ceremony.

I should have known from the beginning that going back in the military was a mistake and that the dream of flying was a whim, not a dedicated lifestyle decision. I dreamed of being a medevac pilot and rescuing soldiers in combat. It was unrealistic because the army could not guarantee which helicopter or which job I would get. I was gambling that I would get exactly what I wanted—drawing to an inside straight. I didn't heed the recurring combat nightmares I had before going to flight school (detailed in my story "Kill Tanks!" in the first *Timeless* book).

Making it through the program wasn't about becoming a pilot as much as it was about being an officer and living in a dreamlike fantasy. I thought being an officer would be different than being enlisted. Surviving flight school was all about not quitting or acknowledging that I had made the wrong decision. I wanted to be an officer and a gentleman—a medevac pilot. I didn't want to end up in the combat arms. I didn't want to kill people, I wanted to save them. I thought flight school was a method for me to get the security of being in the military, but not having the same hassles as being enlisted because I would be a warrant officer. When I got out of the army in 1981, it was a difficult transition. In many ways I had been institutionalized. My decision to re-enter the military was based on my feeling unmoored and directionless in civilian life and hoping that I could fulfill this dream of being an officer. My stubbornness in hanging on to this dream helped me endure the torture I was subjected to and the pain of a yearlong hell in flight school, but my stubbornness also got me into the predicament in the first place. Being an officer wasn't that much different than being enlisted. Same bullshit at a different level. My guardian angel had to work full time to keep me out of trouble and avoid a complete disaster in my life. I had so many more lessons to learn.

WHOLE LOTTA SHAKIN' (1983)

Some of the women I've been in relationships with have cheated on me. How do I know this? Well, I caught one of them in the act, with my best friend no less. On the other occasions, I had circumstantial evidence, overheard some things, or caught momentary glimpses of inappropriate behavior. However, what ties all these incidents together is that I began shaking violently—even my teeth started chattering—at the moment my significant other was having sex with someone else. I'm not writing this to find sympathy or point blame, I was no saint, and maybe they had every reason to stray from me. What I'm suggesting is that I knew what was going on, I felt it, and my mind and body responded with the uncontrollable shaking. How is this possible?

Many people who study psychic phenomena have noted that clairsentience is the most common psychic ability—many have it and don't realize it. Clairsentience (or clear feeling) is the ability to feel the emotions and energy of other people and entities. Some people with enhanced clairsentient abilities are called empaths. This can present a problem for some people because they can become quickly overwhelmed with their feelings and the energy and emotions of others. Knowing that psychic information is being received via feeling or sensing subtle energies around them, clairsentients are often described as overly sensitive. It's a common mistaken belief that clairsentience is not a paranormal gift; on the contrary, experts hold that it's one of the most common psychic powers. So, how do you know if you are clairsentient?

1. Have you felt discomfort and turned around to find someone staring at you?

2. Are you easily overwhelmed in large crowds or while visiting places with a violent or tragic history?

3. Can you sense the mood of people in a room when you enter?

Clairsentients feel what others are feeling and even absorb those emotions. This process, of course, can cause a stirring of emotions for the clairsentient that may not have originated with them.

Clairsentients are also able to feel physical sensations in their bodies as they take in other people's emotions and energy. So, that is why I begin shaking when I sense my partner is having a clandestine romantic liaison. I've had other clairsentient experiences as well. Some say that you know when people are talking about you because you can feel it in your body. I sense it in my ears, manifesting itself in a slight twitching in one ear usually. Chinese folklore suggests that this indicates something generally good will happen—riches, romance, etc. It depends on which ear though, and the time of day.

The first time I noticed my body shaking related to a girlfriend cheating on me came while I was stationed in West Germany. My girlfriend and I fought, and she left to go out. I had a feeling she was going to cheat on me. Then the shaking began. I couldn't stop it, so I ran out of the barracks into the dark night and headed to the track about one-quarter of a mile away. It was stormy and raining, but I kept running and running as I wept, and the rain mixed with the tears that ran down my face. There was some thunder and lightning to accompany my anguish as the heavens opened up in a deluge. It was magical, and powerful, but I was completely heartbroken because I knew what was happening. Later, my girlfriend admitted that she had slept with someone while she was out that tempestuous evening.

Some years later, my girlfriend disappeared from the bed in the middle of the night. I woke up and was shaking violently in the bed. My teeth were chattering. I couldn't sleep, and I waited for her to return. When she did, at about three o'clock in the morning, I confronted her. She claimed that she had gone for a drive and got stuck in a ditch. She waited until a passing truck stopped and towed her out. Sure.

Several years later and still in the US Army, my best friend came to stay with my girlfriend and me for a few weeks while he looked for an apartment in Enterprise, Alabama. We had a barbeque the day he arrived, and later that night I went to bed and left my friend and my girlfriend in the living room. I woke up and was shaking. Something was wrong. I thought I was sick. My teeth were chattering like I was freezing. Then I realized what it was. How could I be so stupid? There had been warning signs, but I ignored them. Was my best friend and my girlfriend having sex in the living room while I was sleeping?

I heard couch springs creaking in the living room in a rhythmic pattern. Among these creaking noises were moans. It was unmistakable what those moans meant, but I had to be sure. I could hear both male and female moaning. I got out of bed and crawled through the window to the backyard. Then I crept around to the living room window and peaked in. Between the drawn window blind slats, I saw something that severely damaged my family's sanctuary, my manhood, and my self-esteem. I felt powerless, helpless, and I was shaking so violently that my teeth chattered. There on my couch sat my best friend with my girlfriend on her knees in front of him with her head in his lap. She would occasionally look around, nervously. He had his hands inside her shirt. They continued to moan. I had seen and heard enough. I went back into the bedroom through the window and lay in bed waiting. I decided to call out.

"Honey, where are you?" I yelled. I heard the couch springs strain as they both stood up suddenly.

"I'm in here darling, we're still talking," she said.

Yeah, they're talking all right, I thought. I heard them say goodnight then she came into the bedroom and took off her clothes and got in bed. I confronted her with what I saw. She denied it and said she was just kissing him and was tired, so her head drooped down into his lap. I interrogated her about the other times I was suspicious, but she didn't say anything. I was ready to beat up my friend and my girlfriend knew that I was about to act.

"No Bruce," she said, "don't hurt him, I'll ask him to leave in the morning."

"He leaves now, or I might really hurt him," I said in a menacingly calm voice. I was angered even more by my girlfriend's defense of this asshole. She jumped out of bed and put on a robe. I heard them arguing and her crying, and then I heard the front door slam as he left. She came back to our room, and I was busy tearing up pictures of my friend that I had. I saw only red. My girlfriend returned to the bed and we lay in tension-filled silence. I would not be in my right mind for quite some time. A few weeks later, one of my other friends from flight school wrote to me from his duty station in Korea. He wrote that my girlfriend had tried to have sex with him one night when she offered him a ride home. He was able to say no. He was afraid that by telling me I probably would never want to be his friend again. He was wrong. I admired his honesty and courage.

There have been two other shaking incidents with different women cheating on me, but I won't belabor the point. I may have deserved the infidelity because of my own dalliances and indiscretions. What goes around comes around. The key point is the amazing psychic phenomena of clairsentience during all these events that led to the same reaction in my mind and body. I was connected and could feel the emotions and energy of the betrayal. So, my friends, if your significant other is out and about and you start shaking violently, they may be tripping the light fantastic with someone else. There is also a possibility that you're coming down with a nasty case of the flu. Either way, it's not good.

RAVEN (1990)

It was early April 1990, and I had just arrived home from school on a sunny, crisp day. My wife Anna looked like she had seen a ghost and was in tears.

"Your mom has cancer," she said bluntly.

"No," I said as I pushed passed her to get to the phone. My shaky fingers pushed in the phone number that I grew up with and that I'll never forget: 206-363-4512. Before we had area codes, we had prefix names attached to our phone numbers. Ours was Emerson 3, 4512, or usually written as EM 3-4512. Emerson referred to the telephone exchange in Seattle that serviced our number. Each exchange could only handle 100,000 phone numbers.

"I just got my death sentence. Looks like it's the 'Big C,'" my mom said.

It took me a few seconds to process what she meant. A shroud of gloom came over me. I remembered that she had complained of feeling weak and had gone to the doctor a few times before.

"I thought the doctor said it was pneumonia?"

"The doctor was wrong," she said. I don't remember the rest of the conversation. My mother had been diagnosed with colon cancer. Her cancer had metastasized and spread to her liver, lungs, and other organs. Terminal cancer in other words.

The semester was almost over at Bowling Green State University, in Bowling Green, Ohio, where I had just started the first year of my history doctoral program. I was able to carve out a few days at the end of April to fly up to Seattle and see mom, but then I had to be back on Monday, April 30th, for finals. Her cancer was spreading quickly and making her weaker by the day. I was at the Group Health Hospital in Redmond, Washington, visiting with Mom when her doctor arrived in her room. Mom was sitting up in bed and smiling as he entered. The doctor looked at her, looked back at his patient status clipboard, and then again at my mom.

"Well, I expected to see a very sick lady in this room, but you seem very strong! I thought I had the wrong room," he said cheerfully.

"I'm tough, I'm a Viking," my mom said, beaming with pride. Later, she demanded that the surgeon operate and remove the original tumor in her colon. He told her that it wouldn't do any good and might hasten her death.

"I don't care, I want that devil out of me!" she said. The operation and anesthesia were hard on her, and she emerged from the procedure even weaker. There was nothing more the hospital could do for her, and she was told she could go home with a hospice nurse. On Sunday, April 29th, my mom was transported home by ambulance. My brother Alf and I drove on ahead while my father rode with Mom in the ambulance.

As we drove up the long steep driveway from 55th Avenue Northeast in Kenmore, Washington, where I grew up, I reminisced about the four houses Mom and Dad had lived in on either side of that driveway. The original house at the bottom left-hand side, the little house above that, which my father built for my great uncle Martin, and the brown house at the top of the hill where I grew up, built by my father. My father built two more houses on the right-hand side of the long driveway, beautiful custom homes. The second home from the top on the right-hand side was where they were living in 1990. Driving past all of these houses was like a tour of our life in America, of my life growing up. As we pulled into the short parking driveway of their house, we noticed a large raven on the front steps. The front steps were framed by Rhododendron bushes on either side. That raven was just standing there, not afraid of us. As we got out of the car, he squawked, loudly, a harsh grating type sound, then he flew off to the North. It was a beautiful, sunny day, and you could see the Cascade Mountains and especially Mt. Rainier. This was the view I grew up with in Kenmore.

"Did you see that big crow?" my brother asked.

"It was a raven," I said.

"Yeah, you're right," he said. According to mythology in most parts of the world, the raven is a bird of ill omen and a foreteller of bad weather and impending death. The raven is also considered a messenger of the Great Spirit in Native American folklore. A group of ravens is known as a murder. In Norse mythology, which my mother taught us as children, the raven was a most revered symbol and messenger carrier of Odin, the chief god in the Norse pantheon. Odin was always accompanied by a pair of ravens, Hugin (thought) and Munin (memory), who would fly around the world to bring news to Odin. In the Old Testament, the raven is the first bird Noah sent to look for land.

As my brother and I watched the raven fly away making his other-worldly gurgling croaking sound, we both knew what his presence meant, although we didn't say it.

"You ever saw a raven on the steps before?" I asked my brother.

"No, they stay in the woods not by houses; they're usually up in the mountains," he said.

After a minute or two, the ambulance arrived with Mom and Dad. We helped get Mom comfortable in her bed and met the hospice nurse who would attend her and help Dad. We didn't tell Mom and Dad about the raven. It was time for me to go. I hugged my mom and told her that I loved her, something I didn't usually say. I wasn't sure that she heard me anyway. She was happy to be home, although she was in tremendous pain, I could see it. I held back my tears. Norwegians are a stoic bunch. I had to get back to Ohio for finals week. My brother drove me to the airport. It was a quiet drive.

Finals week went well, and I got daily status reports from my brother and sister Bjørg. On Thursday night I called my mother.

"Mom, I give my last final exam tomorrow and then we'll be done for the semester, and I'll fly back up to see you."

"Don't jeopardize your job," she said.

"I won't."

"No hurry, I'm just laying here," she said.

"In your own bed," I said.

"Ya, good to be home," she said.

"You're the best mom in the whole world, and I love you," I said as I choked up and almost dropped the phone. Mom laughed a little.

"Thank you," she said. My parents never told me that they loved me. I knew that they did love me, but they never said the words. They were from the old world. They figured the love they had for their children would be self-evident through their providing food, clothing, a roof over your head, and safety. That was the last time I spoke to my mom. Early in the morning on May 4th, 1990, I walked to school and gave my last final. When I returned, Anna met me in the doorway.

"Your mom died," she said in her usual blunt manner, but with tears in her eyes. She was also the product of immigrant, old world, tough love parents. I collapsed into the overstuffed chair in the living room and tears formed in the corners of my eyes. The boys were still at school. I thought to myself that my childhood was over. I was without my mother. Being a historian, I noted that my mom died precisely twenty years after four young student protesters were killed by equally young National Guardsmen at Kent State University in Ohio. Tragic events, both. My mother was a tough Viking woman, and it was altogether fitting and symbolic that the raven showed up on her doorstep. He was there as a messenger and reminder that we're all Vikings and should live our lives fearlessly and with honor. My mom would want it that way.

SEA EAGLE (1992)

I was combing through the Norwegian government archives and conducting research for my doctoral dissertation in the Spring of 1992 in Norway. I stayed with my Nazi aunt in Oslo and for the most part it was a successful venture. I wasn't feeling well and had not felt well since starting graduate school in January 2000. This period of ill health was made worse after my arrest and separation from my first wife and estrangement from my two older boys. I had lost 50 pounds due to stress and anxiety. It was a strange time in my life.

After finishing my research in the capitol city of Oslo, I flew up to Northern Norway, to Andøya, where my father was living. I enjoy being up North more than being in Oslo. It's more peaceful and feels like home to me. It was during this visit that my father took me on a historical walk that I documented in a story called "Coffee Cups and Vikings" in my first *Timeless* book. My cousin Ole invited me to take a hike up to the mountain above the village of Åse where we have our traditional farmhouse where my father was born. Ole was used to walking in the mountains and was a dairy farmer by trade. It was hard to keep up with him. We took a northern route up the mountain and passed by a high cliff area known as Haukhamran overlooking a large lake called Ånesvatnet. The cliff plunged hundreds of feet down and it made me dizzy to stand near the edge. As I was walking carefully near the cliff side, I noticed a large feather. I picked up the feather and Ole said: "It is an eagle feather!"

"What kind of eagle?"

"A sea eagle," said Ole.

I couldn't believe my luck, I had never found an eagle feather before and I knew that they were rare and considered sacred objects by many different cultures in the world. As I basked in my good fortune, I could see the other side of the island, the open ocean side. It was a beautiful sunny day without much wind. All seemed right with the world and my burdens seemed lighter as we continued on our hike.

Sea eagles, also known as white-tailed eagles, are found in Eurasia with most nesting pairs living on the coast of Norway. They are a close cousin of the bald eagle. Sea eagles can weigh up to 16 pounds and can have a wingspan of eight feet. That's a big bird! Local island legends say that sea eagles have been known to take newborn lambs and carry them away. Some legends even say that sea eagles have swooped down and grabbed babies in their sharp talons. Not surprisingly, many local people are frightened of them.

I asked my cousin Merete about eagles and their place in the culture. To Northern Norwegians, eagles symbolize strength, perspective, and a connection between our world and the spirit world. It's considered a strong and powerful animal. Many feel empowered when they see an eagle. The feathers give one the power of the eagle. Merete told me about a little girl on Andøya who was playing outside in her yard when she was taken by an eagle in the 1950s. She was later found in a crevice in the mountain side and her dress was torn in many places, presumably by eagle talons. She is still alive today to tell the tale. My cousin Trond was attacked by an eagle when he was wearing a bright red winter cap. The eagle swooped down and stole his hat. Merete nearly had her puppy taken by an eagle. It's said that eagles take many small lambs and small dogs, especially in January when they are most hungry. On Bleiksøya (also known as the puffin island), there is a tour that leaves from the village of Bleik on the north end of the island. Tourists are often horrified when eagles suddenly swoop down and grab the little comical, orange, black, and white puffins.

In the United States, eagles are protected under two federal laws: The Bald and Golden Eagle Protection Act, and the Migratory Bird Treaty Act. Of course, it's illegal to kill eagles, but these laws also prohibit the possession, use, and sale of eagle feathers and other parts of the eagles. The US Fish and Wildlife Service understands the religious and cultural significance of eagles to Native Americans and works with tribes to provide them with eagle feathers for religious use. To Native Americans, the feather symbolizes trust, honor, strength, wisdom, power, freedom, and more. It's a great honor if an Indian has been given an eagle feather. Indians believe that eagles have a special connection with the heavens since they fly so high and are messengers from the Creator. Eagle feathers must be cared for and never dropped (like the reverence one has for a national flag). You must perform a brave deed to earn an eagle feather. Eagles are said to carry the prayers of man between the earth and the spirit world where the Creator lives. In Norse mythology, the eagle is a symbol of strength. Odin had one eagle and two ravens at his side. An eagle also sits at the top of Yggdrasil, the World Tree.

With all the important symbolic reverence for eagles, I felt extremely privileged to have the feather in my possession. When we arrived at Ole's cabin by a small lake named Dalvatnet to have lunch and something to drink, I noticed that the eagle feather was gone. So were my sunglasses. I looked everywhere and even retraced my steps for some of the way. Nothing. I had lost the sacred eagle feather, and my sunglasses. I wasn't so worried about my sunglasses, even though they were nice, I lose sunglasses all the time. The eagle feather was what I was really upset about. What did it mean? Would the good luck go away? Had I committed sacrilege, and now would I be visited with bad luck? I was very unhappy.

Bad luck ensued. I lost custody of my two older boys and we grew apart, my illness continued and even got worse, and I almost died from an abscessed tooth that went septic. Although I was able to complete my doctorate in 1993, a dark cloud hung over me and any relationship I tried to establish. My temper got worse and I was even more unhappy. If only I had hung on to the eagle feather, or maybe, not even found it in the first place. It could be that I didn't earn the right to have the eagle feather. Maybe someday I'll earn another one.

THE NEVER-ENDING RIVER (1992)

One day in the Fall of 1992, tired from a hard day's work at Seattle Central Community College, I sat down at home and began to daydream. The daydream turned into a vision of me standing on the shore of a never-ending river. It was early in the morning and mist rose from the river. The tranquil sound of the water running over the smooth rocks at its surface comforted me. On the opposite side of the river, I noticed two shadowy figures approaching, but I couldn't make them out. As they came closer, I recognized them as Dr. Martin Luther King, Jr., and Mohandas K. Gandhi.

"Hey, can I talk to you?" I asked. They acknowledged me with shared smiles and nods as they stopped walking.

"I would really like to talk with both of you," I said. But then I began to feel uncomfortable as I realized that I wasn't in familiar surroundings. "Where are we anyway?" I asked.

"We simply exist in this place where you happen to be," said King.

"Are we in heaven?" I asked with a puzzled look on my face.

Gandhi smiled and looked at King. "We have moved beyond the existence you know. The spirit is eternal and will always be. The body is merely a vessel. Once it is spent, you return to the universe from whence you came," explained Gandhi. I was feeling overwhelmed by these two historic figures and was trying to understand the meanings of their words.

"You both believed in non-violence, but is violence ever justified?" I asked.

"Violence begets violence. It is cyclical. A violent act is followed by counterviolence and so on," said Gandhi.

"Violence isn't only physical. Deprive a person of life, liberty, and the pursuit of happiness and you've also committed violence," added King.

"What if I'm attacked," I asked, "should I just let someone kill me?"

"You assume that the attacker wishes to kill. If you counterattack and kill him, what if he only wanted your pocket change? Being prepared to kill only encourages killing. Look for trouble and you will find it," explained Gandhi.

"The heart of your adversary or oppressor can be changed with the power of love, not violence," added King.

"How do I know for sure what will happen?" I asked.

Gandhi smiled, then looked at King who smiled in return. "You do not know. You only know yourself, and it is there that true nonviolence begins—with yourself," answered Gandhi.

I wanted to dig deeper. "What if I'm killed? How will that accomplish anything?" I asked.

King turned to Gandhi for a moment and both nodded their heads.

"I know what you are thinking, both of us were shot to death," said Gandhi.

"Exactly," I said.

"If you're shot then you move on to another existence. You'll have stood your ground and stopped the cycle of violence so that others may learn. The power of one person is great," added King.

"And we live on in spirit. Are we not still of value to you, alive in thought and idea, even though our physical bodies have turned to dust?" asked Gandhi.

"I don't understand," I said.

Gandhi's smile turned to a very serious look as he was about to speak. "It is not entirely your fault. Society does not teach bravery, but cowardice. A fully armed man is a coward at heart. The possession of arms implies an element of fear if not cowardice. True nonviolence is an impossibility without the possession of unadulterated fearlessness," said Gandhi. There was a pause as I thought about their wisdom.

Both men turned toward each other and seemed to indicate that it was time to go.

"Wait," I said. "I've got more questions."

"It's time for you to return to your existence and continue the struggle for peace," King said.

I looked at these two great men and shook my head. "But I'm not brave enough, I'm afraid," I said.

"Do not despair," Gandhi said, "the power of love is great and will carry you like a giant wave once you have accepted it. The work to be done is difficult, but the reward is a world of hope and peace."

"But there is so much anger, hatred, and war," I said.

King looked at me with great intensity. "And all of that is due to violence in all of its forms. In the age of guided missiles and misguided men, scientific power has outrun moral power," King said. Then, he stretched his arms out wide as if to encompass the boundlessness of this dreamscape. "We live in a world house, a family unduly separated in ideas, culture, and interest, who, because we can never again live apart, must learn to live with each other in peace," he said.

Gandhi smiled at King and then they began to walk away and disappeared into the mist of the faraway shore. I stood there for a moment listening to the river and breathing in deeply. As my vision ended and I returned to the reality of the day, I began to cry both tears of joy and tears of sadness.

DAVID AND THE DUKE (1997)

Sitting on the grass on the Green River Community College campus one day in the Spring of 1997, I was daydreaming when I suddenly had a vision of John Wayne. He was walking right through the campus, and no one seemed to recognize or notice him. John Wayne had died in 1979. He acted as if he owned the place. John Wayne looked great—his tanned leathery skin reflected the bright sunlight. He wasn't entirely normal in appearance—he had a shimmering glow about him. It was a warm day, and John Wayne was sauntering in his usual way. He cut diagonally across my path toward the Performing Arts building. He looked fit and trim in jeans and a plain white sports shirt. Someone finally recognized him and approached. The person who stopped him looked out of place, she wore 1970s clothes and was cast in the same strange light as John Wayne.

"When are you going to teach again, Mr. Wayne?" she asked. Stopping to look at the woman, John Wayne's face wrinkled into a sideways smile as he cocked his head slightly.

"Soon, a few weeks," he said, "we are meeting as the Committee of 77 right now, have to go, sorry ma'am."

I wasn't sure what he meant by the Committee of 77, but later I did some research and found out that the first law enforcement organization in the Montana Territory was the Vigilance Committee formed on March 7, 1877, in Virginia City, Montana. Montana State Troopers have 3-7-77 on their shoulder patches. Interestingly, the first Masonic Lodge in Montana was founded on March 7, 1877, in Bannock, Montana.

John Wayne headed into the Performing Arts building. Why was John Wayne haunting our campus? I had been assigned to the 82nd Airborne Division in Ft. Bragg, North Carolina, and had seen the John Wayne exhibit at the Special Forces Museum. John Wayne had filmed part of his 1968 film *Green Berets* at Ft. Bragg. I had felt a connection to John Wayne having grown up with his war and western movies. But then it occurred to me, John Wayne's appearance on our campus was probably because of my friend David Willson, a Vietnam veteran and novelist who worked as a reference librarian at Green River Community College. He was quite the John Wayne aficionado. I was certain that he had more John Wayne memorabilia than anyone in the world. It was safe to say that David was obsessed with the Duke.

"John Wayne was the reason many of us went to war in Vietnam. We were trying to live up to his standards of manhood," David would often say. Maybe his zealous fandom had drawn John Wayne's spirit from its place of rest and left it wandering around our campus—as if our campus wasn't weird enough already. I was no stranger to ghosts, as they had always been part of my life. David was my best friend, so I figured that it was the least I could do to help him exorcise this particular ghost.

Still within my dream vision, I walked into David's office and threw myself down in his 1950s-style TV chair. His office was filled to the brim with videos, films, books, papers, posters, old typewriters— like a used bookstore crammed into one small room. It was no wonder a movie star ghost would be attracted to this campus—David's office was a Mecca for wandering film spirits.

"Saw a ghost today," I said.

Dropping his book review magazine suddenly to his lap, David stared at me, raising one eyebrow slowly, then the other. "So, imagine that, a ghost here at the college. You do indeed have a gimlet eye," he said in a rather mocking tone.

"Come on David, you know about it, you brought him here I'm sure. Now, the question is, what are we going to do about Mr. John Wayne's ghost?" I asked.

David turned around in his chair and faced the stack of books directly behind him.

"*We* are not going to do anything, I'm comfortable with him being here, and I don't want anything to change," he said with his voice rising in volume at the end.

"Well, it can't be healthy having this ghost wandering around, I mean, he could scare the hell out of someone, give them a heart attack or something," I said as David suddenly interrupted me.

"And if this does happen," he said as he sprang to his feet, "if he does scare someone to death, whose fault would it be? Certainly, not mine, who could find me guilty just for having built a shrine to John Wayne? I have no control over his ghost. However, if someone were to die from fright, just theoretically speaking of course, it would be a perfect crime, don't you think?" he asked. He was pacing back and forth now in the narrow confines of his office.

I looked at David suspiciously; he had sat down again, but now he was looking up at the ceiling, hands folded on his stomach, as a narrow smile worked its way slowly across his face.

"Psychic crime is still a crime. The only judge that matters is the one in your own conscience," I said.

His expression changed dramatically. He looked at me angrily. "Don't you go and mess this up, if you are a true friend you will sit by quietly and let the ghost do his work. Those who would be hurt are fully deserving of their fate, I assure you," he said as the smile returned to his face.

I left David's office and went back outside to sit on the park bench by the outdoor theater. I wanted to help David, but I had the feeling that John Wayne's ghost needed to return to its resting place, and that David needed to give up his plan of revenge. Just then, the Duke appeared from behind the bushes and sat down next to me.

"What's the problem there, pilgrim?" he asked.

"You startled me, Mr. Wayne; I was just thinking about what to do here. I want to help my friend. You see, he thinks that maybe you will scare some of the people he hates here at the college, perhaps even scare them to death," I said as John Wayne looked at me intensely.

"Here's what you do fella. If he's really your friend, then you gotta help him so that he doesn't get hurt, and so others don't get hurt," he said.

"But wait Mr. Wayne, you were in all those westerns and war movies, I thought that you were into war and violence and all that stuff?" I asked.

John Wayne stood up and put one of his booted feet on the bench. "I don't glorify war or killing; I don't want people to think that. I want peace for the world, and especially for my country, I want us to be at peace. My message is simple: Fight and defend yourself only when necessary. We should seek methods other than violence whenever possible. I'm worried about your friend David, but he won't listen to me," he said.

"You mean he brought you here, but he doesn't hear you?" I asked.

"He hears, he just doesn't listen. He's a good man, but war has haunted him and his family for generations, he needs to find peace," said John Wayne.

"It just seems odd that John Wayne would be helping someone find peace," I said.

"Only Nixon could go to China, right?" said Wayne as he turned to go.

"Wait, Mr. Wayne," I started to ask but didn't finish because John Wayne was gone. I sat there for a few seconds in disbelief, then, suddenly, a shiver of self-realization shocked my body, and I awoke from my daydream. My dream vision had played itself out, and I had apparently been walking around and was sitting on the bench like in my vision. Oh shit, maybe someone saw me talking to no one and would think I was crazy. I could lose my job. Of course, it would be okay if they saw John Wayne too, but I could not be sure of that. I quickly looked around. No one had been watching, but two students were lying on the grass. They were making out and not paying attention, so I was safe. I had to go and talk to David about all this; it wasn't going to be easy. By the way, John Wayne was a Freemason, and David's great, great uncle was on the Vigilance Committee of 77 in Virginia City, Montana in 1877. Another interesting synchronicity.

THE PROGENITOR (1997)

One of my favorite comedians was Richard Pryor. He once told a story about getting caught red-handed while cheating on his wife. When his wife walked in and found him in bed with another woman, Richard looked at his wife with mock incredulity and said: "Who ya gonna believe? Me or your lyin' eyes?"

Seeing is believing, right? Since I was a little boy, I've wanted there to be life on other planets and wanted to meet an alien. Growing up with *Lost in Space, Star Trek,* and a plethora of Saturday afternoon science-fiction movies, I desperately wanted us not to be alone in the universe. The Apollo space program and moon landing in July 1969 further fueled this passion for outer space, the final frontier. Spock, from the original *Star Trek* TV series, was and still is my favorite TV character. Later, in the 1980s, I was inspired by Carl Sagan's *Cosmos* TV series. I've researched Area 51 in Nevada, and Hangar 18, the top-secret part of Wright Patterson Air Force Base in Dayton, Ohio, where, coincidentally, my eldest son works. All of this fascinates me. In high school I read Erich von Däniken's *Chariots of the Gods?* which was published in 1968. In that book he made claims about extraterrestrial influences on early human culture. The legacy of his book and the controversy it stirred in the scientific community continues today with many ancient astronaut hypotheses and TV shows like *Ancient Aliens.* There are those people who make fun of those who believe in aliens and the paranormal, but the number of people who believe and relate their experiences just continues to grow in the world. I have experience, so it's really not a matter of belief. It reminds me of the words generally attributed to German philosopher Arthur Schopenhauer. To paraphrase: All truth passes through three stages. First, it is ridiculed. Second, it is violently opposed. Third, it is accepted as being self-evident.

The former head of the Advanced Aerospace Threat Identification Program at the Pentagon, Luis Elizondo, investigated phenomena reported and collected by military service members. Elizondo described some of the objects that they studied: "Things that don't have any obvious flight surfaces, any obvious forms of propulsion, and moving in ways that include extreme maneuverability beyond, I would submit, the healthy g-forces of any human or anything biological." The major news media outlets released video captured by now-retired US Navy pilot David Fravor. He saw and filmed a UFO off the coast of Southern California in 2004. Appearing on CNN, Fravor said it was a "white object, oblong, pointing north, moving erratically. As I got close to it ... it rapidly accelerated to the south and disappeared in less than two seconds."

Elizondo explained that the Advanced Aerospace Threat Identification Program concluded that these UFOs, "...are displaying characteristics that are not currently within the US inventory, nor in any foreign inventory...there is very compelling evidence that we may not be alone." I've never seen a UFO. I was, however, contacted by what I believe were alien beings. In fact, we may be standing on the brink of full and open contact with extraterrestrial life.

One day in 1997, I met an ancient being in one of my visions. I believe that I may have been chosen to help us prepare for contact. I'll get back to that story in a moment. First, an explanation of what I mean by visions. I'm not asleep, but I'm not fully awake when I experience a vision. I'm in a middle state of consciousness. Scientists call this the alpha brain wave state. I hear and see, but not in an ordinary sense. I straddle a doorway between two realities, two worlds that coexist but aren't always apparent to one another. It was in such a state of mind that I met the Progenitor. The language I heard in the vision was English, but I can't be sure that it was. I understood perfectly in the vision, but when I tried to write down what I heard, it seemed as if it was in some unrecognizable language. I must think about what I've heard first, and then write it out in standard English. The Progenitor was standing with eyes closed, hands folded, wearing a light beige colored tunic made from some coarse fiber. His face wasn't Homo Sapien, it was australopithecine and ashen, with narrow set eyes. It was clear to me that he was the first and original mystic, but he couldn't have been a proto-human, I suspect he was of alien origin.

After Earth's millions of revolutions around the sun and the billions of people that have come before me, I was chosen to receive a message beyond time from this ancient seer. The Progenitor drifted through dimensional doorways and appeared to be revolving in space. He then spoke to me in a peaceful, contemplative manner.

"I'm the Progenitor," the primordial mystic said. It was a simple message, but it was almost beyond my imagination to be receiving such an important communication.

"I speak to you through the portal of the past, future, and present, all as one, and one as all," he explained.

"Why me? Why are you speaking to me? What do I have to offer?" I asked.

"The answer reveals itself as a seed silently planted that grows," he said.

I thought deeply about his words.

"You are one in a long line of seers," he continued.

"Who would believe me?" I asked.

"Believe or not believe; it's experience that teaches. You must be the connector, the bridge-builder. There have been many messages through time with different messengers, and all are pointing to the same obvious truth," he said with a rising tone in his voice.

"I understand," I said. My body was tingling from the excitement of making this contact.

The Progenitor continued, still revolving in space. "Both deliverance and peace come from knowing this as one cannot exist without the other. The bargain for life is death, the bargain for peace is war, the bargain for happiness is sorrow, the bargain for health is sickness, the bargain for wealth is poverty, and the bargain for love is hate," he said.

I sensed that I was leaving my body and drifting through space with him as I listened intently to his words of wisdom.

"Lament the day passing, but the night will still come. I offer this gift, from the beyond, through a channel with many faces, a seed planted in the womb of the earth," he said as he continued to rotate in outer space. "The great unknown lies beyond the veil of death. It's yet another beginning. Look at the black hole. What do you see? Light does not escape. It's what you don't see that is most important. The universe pours through the rips in time and space. A quasar explodes on the other side, yet you may not see it. You see the past and the future, from infinity to infinity, with no real beginning and no real end," he said.

"I think I understand, but, where are you? Are you an alien? So many questions," I said. And then he was gone, and the vision was done.

I was afraid to tell people about my experience. I finally told one of my colleagues in 1999; she was an anthropology professor. I described the Progenitor and showed her the picture I had drawn of him. She listened politely.

"You're a pretty spacey dude, Bruce," she said as she smiled and was busy filing papers at her desk. She stopped filing and looked at me directly.

"But he can't be australopithecine; they didn't have language. Language only developed 100,000 years ago, and Australopithecus was extinct two million years ago," she said. I didn't bring it up again with her and didn't share my experience with anyone else until now.

According to Noam Chomsky, Massachusetts Institute of Technology (MIT) professor of linguistics, a single chance mutation occurred in one individual about 100,000 years ago. This mutation triggered the instantaneous emergence of language ability. This random genetic change in a single individual then spread to the rest of the group and beyond.

This mutation triggered the instantaneous emergence of language ability. This random genetic change in a single individual then spread to the rest of the group and beyond. Chomsky defined the concept of "Discrete Infinity" as the property by which human language is constructed from a few dozen discrete parts and then combine in an infinite variety of expressions of thought, imagination, and feeling. It's a unique property of human language. Human computational ability also took a giant leap at about the same time as language. We went from only being able to count up to a fixed number to be able to count indefinitely. Could this have been the work of aliens contacting early humans? Could they have given us this evolutionary boost? Could the Progenitor have taken his physical form during the initial contact with Australopithecus and later returned to provide us with the gift of language? I don't know, but what I do know is that I was contacted.

The possibility of alien contact had always been there for me, just waiting, somewhere over the rainbow bridge, Bifrost in Norse mythology. Being of Norwegian heritage, I grew up with Norse mythology and stories of Vikings. Bifrost, that burning rainbow bridge that connects Asgard, the world of the gods, with Midgard, the world of humanity here on Earth, makes sense to me. I'm a bridgebuilder and guardian, like Heimdall, the ever-vigilant god who is the guardian of the rainbow bridge. I stand ready to open the bridge, so our world can make contact with the world of the Progenitor. Unlike Richard Pryor in his funny story, I've done nothing wrong; I'm just sharing what I've experienced. I understand the skepticism and the comfort that comes with not wanting to believe or accept that we're not alone in the universe. A recent YouGov poll revealed that 54 percent of Americans believe that intelligent alien life exists. We've been taught to believe only what our eyes can see, but there is more. To see the quantum universe as it really is, you must look beyond what we call normal, everyday reality. It comes down to this: Who are you going to believe? Quantum reality, or your lying eyes?

AMERICAN CORNERS (2003)

It all started rather innocently. I was awarded a Fulbright teaching and research award in 2003. I was proud to be one of only 600 educators selected that year to travel abroad and teach my designated subject. My country was Norway, and my host institution was the University of Tromsø in Northern Norway. I was a natural selection for the Fulbright Committee because I spoke Norwegian and had traveled to Norway extensively. Accompanying me were my wife Heather (now ex-wife) and my two young children. But I had already foreshadowed this happening back in 1995.

In 1995, I had just ended one relationship and was headlong into another one. My girlfriend Heather accompanied me to Norway while I was conducting research for a book on women leaders. I had set up several interviews in Oslo including an interview with Grete Berget, the Norwegian Minister of Families and Children. I also tried to meet Erna Solberg, the leader of the Conservative Party in Norway. I had met Erna in 1994 when she was a keynote speaker at the Women's Leadership Conference I had helped organize at Green River Community College in Auburn, Washington. I didn't have a chance to meet with Erna in 1995, but I talked to her on the phone. I reminded her that while she was visiting in Seattle, I predicted that she would one day be Prime Minister. She laughed then and laughed again this time. In 2013, she did become Prime Minister of Norway. When I visited with her in 2016 along with my wife Ginger, I reminded Erna again of my prediction. She didn't remember.

My two sons Bjørn and Byron flew to Norway to meet me and Heather after my research was completed in the Summer of 1995. We then traveled to Northern Norway to stay at our old farm home in Åse, on the island of Andøya. My father was still alive in 1995 and lived half of the year in Norway and the other half in Seattle. We borrowed Dad's 1986 Mazda and drove five hours to Tromsø. We wanted to look around, and I wanted to visit the University of Tromsø. While we were visiting the campus, I told Heather, and the boys that I was going to get a teaching job in Norway and I hoped that it was at the University of Tromsø. I could already see myself having an office there and teaching. It would be my dream come true.

When I arrived in Tromsø in 2003, I visited the university and was introduced to the staff and shown to my office (a large open room with a huge window facing the courtyard). I had seen this office before in 1995 when I predicted that I would one-day work there. The office manager told me that my teaching schedule would be two classes, one with five graduate students, the other with 20 undergraduates. My Norwegian colleagues said that two classes constituted a heavy load. I could only laugh since I regularly have seven classes and over 300 students per semester at Citrus College where I teach. We stayed with our Canadian friend and her family until the university found us a lovely two-bedroom, two-story condo.

After a few days of getting oriented to our new residence and the city, I was introduced to my teaching assistant (TA) who was also the wife of one of the professors. They were American expatriates. I got a weird feeling about them, once again my intuition at work. Not long after the semester began, I was hearing stories from my graduate students about how these American expatriates were plotting behind my back. They thought that I posed a threat to them since they were vying for a permanent position at the university. My TA was secretly passing on my instructional materials to her husband who was passing them on to a friend in the administration. She also made up stories about my being late or not doing what I was supposed to do in the classroom. I was having weird dreams about spies and living a shadow life. For a town of only 50,000 people, there was certainly a lot of drama. I even wrote a song about my experiences in Tromsø called "Ghost Man."

> Hello out there, as you're floating in the air
>
> Flying so high, everywhere
>
> I can't help it, but I just have to stare
>
> You're not here you're not there
>
> Hey ghost man, are you forgotten and alone

Living life without a home

Afraid to leave, and waiting by the phone

We then had a Fulbright orientation in Oslo, the capital city. It was there that I first met the US embassy personnel. One of them was the head of the Political and Economic Section, and the other was a Norwegian national named ▇ who served as his executive assistant. My immediate impression of ▇ was that he was a CIA agent. His demeanor was somewhat gruff, and he had a swagger—not typical for most Norwegians. His first appearance was when the Political Section Chief was briefing us. ▇ dropped a large box of booklets on the table behind us with a resounding crash. Everyone was startled, and he smiled in delight.

The Political Section Chief mentioned that he wanted to work with us in our capacities as academic ambassadors. I contacted the embassy several weeks later and spoke to him. He suggested a program called American Corners. I was asked to try to get it set up in Tromsø. One of my Norwegian colleagues informed me that the US government had previously maintained a secret CIA station in Tromsø, but it was shut down when the Norwegians discovered what was going on. The United States has had no intelligence-gathering operation in Tromsø since that time. The Political Section Chief asked me to talk to folks at the university to see if the American Embassy could donate materials to the library and designate part of an area to American cultural studies. The Norwegians immediately met this with skepticism. Later I was put in contact with ▇, the Norwegian National whom I suspected of being a CIA agent. He was blunter than his boss and impressed upon me the importance of establishing this toehold to combat rabid anti-Americanism due to the Bush administration foreign policies and War in Iraq. Although it was becoming more evident what they wanted me to do, I wasn't ready to jump to any conclusions.

It was then that ▇ asked if he could send two embassy officials up to Tromsø to meet with faculty and students. I agreed and set up a forum for discussion of US foreign policy. I was to serve as the host for the two officers. We had a very lively meeting that was well attended.

The young officers had their hands full with questions about the validity of the Bush Doctrine. Afterwards, I invited them to lunch, but they declined because they had to return to Oslo. They asked me about my colleagues; they already knew their names, their political leanings, and more than they should have known. They also knew the two American expatriates who had become my enemies. They impressed upon me the importance of establishing the American Corners.

As fate would have it, we didn't stay the whole academic year. The family that was renting our home in Glendora, California, was late with the rent and then threatened to not pay in January 2004. We didn't have any money saved so we would miss our mortgage payment if they didn't pay their rent. We were working on very narrow financial margins. I had to make the tough decision to return to the United States early. The American expatriates were glad to be rid of me. I never was able to get the toehold the embassy wanted in Tromsø before we left.

Russia is very active in Northern Norway. The strategic importance of Norway's coastline was clear to the Germans who invaded and occupied Norway during World War II. They wanted to control the shipping lanes to the Russian Kola Peninsula and the supply of iron ore coming from Sweden through Narvik in Northern Norway. The Russians understand the continuing strategic importance of Northern Norway.

Our old family farm is on Andøya (200 miles above the Arctic Circle). That island is very strategic, as it juts out into the Norwegian Sea and has a military airbase and submarine surveillance activities. There is also a rocket launch center at the northern end of the island. Recently, a Russian doctor was employed near the airbase and rocket center and has since been deported for espionage activities. All my cousins knew of this long before the Norwegian government acted. There is a former NATO base near the airbase that had been sold to a mysterious Eastern European businessman. All the military buildings and underground bunkers went with the sale. This supposed businessman turned the base into a fishing camp. None of my cousins believed this. The Russian fishermen always show up when there is military training or exercises on the airbase and whenever there is a rocket test from the Andøya Rocket Center at the northern tip of the island—especially when it's a military-related launch involving the United States or our other allies. If you go to the website for the fishing camp, you can see from the photos that these aren't just sports fishermen, these are foreign agents and former KGB men. I couldn't believe how transparent all of this was.

My cousin's husband flies Orion anti-submarine planes from the airbase and says the Russians harass him every time he flies. A fifth column has developed on the island of pro-Russian Norwegians. The latest blow is that the Norwegian government has decided to shut down the military airbase on Andøya and move to Evenes, near Narvik. That would leave Andøya defenseless. Evenes is surrounded by mountains and pilots have great difficulty landing and taking off from there. Historically, Andøya is a very important island since it commands the shipping lanes to the Kola Peninsula. The Germans had over 2000 troops on the island during WWII (my father and mother lived there under Nazi occupation). The island is still strategic today and that is why there is a Russian presence. The Norwegians sold a formerly secret submarine base in Tromsø (northeast of Andøya) to a Russian businessman. It's hidden under a mountain. I couldn't make this up, it's like an old episode of the campy TV series *Batman*.

Later, I discovered that American Corners was a CIA sponsored project. The CIA was interested in Tromsø because of the presence of so many Russians in the city. American Corners was an attempt to establish a front for the CIA to spy on the Russians who were spying on the Norwegians in Northern Norway. Apparently, in trying to get me to establish American Corners, I almost became the CIA's unwitting operative. My intuition was correct, and it wouldn't be the first or last time.

ON A FLIGHT TO DALLAS (2008)

It was February 2008, on a flight to Dallas from Los Angeles that I, for the first time in my life, was flying first class. Seated in front of me were two guys in cowboy hats. One had a white hat and the other a black hat. They were drinking heavily. They looked like rich oil men and they confirmed that when they spoke about drill rigs and oil markets and other oil industry stuff. Now, I don't eavesdrop normally as a habit, but it does sometimes give me fodder for my writing, so I continued to listen. These guys were animated and loud, so I probably couldn't have tuned them out even if I wanted to. As we made our way to Dallas, their conversations turned to politics. Barack Obama was leading in the polls against Hillary Clinton for the Democratic nomination and was running close with Republican John McCain in head-to-head opinion polls. Some political pundits were speculating that Obama might go all the way.

"Do ya think Obama will get nominated?" asked the white hat.

"Yeah, looks like it . . . at least that'll get Hillary to shut up for a spell," said the black hat.

They both laughed and quaffed another drink. Then they thought for a moment and were quiet. I pretended to read my book and continued to listen intently.

"Can he beat McCain?" asked the black hat.

"Yup, could happen," answered the white hat. I was shocked by his answer. What do these guys know? Are rich and powerful people privy to information we don't have? Is the future already laid out for us? Conspiracies of all sorts ran through my head. I could tell that one of the oilmen was bewildered.

"A black man as President?" asked the black hat.

"Yup . . . if he can play ball," answered the white hat. They were quiet for a minute and I was wondering what he meant by that last comment.

"And they all play ball," said the black hat. There was a moment of silence, then both laughed loudly. I guess I shouldn't have been surprised by the racist remark. But, then I thought that it might have been a double entendre. Then there was some silence as both were thinking of what to say next. The few seconds seemed like hours as I craned my neck and positioned my ears to pick up their next utterances. They continued, but much quieter.

"Seriously, ya think Americans will elect a black President?" asked the black hat. They looked at each other. One of them took a big sip and gulped audibly.

"Yeah, but it don't matter. He'll do what he's told to do . . . or else," said the white hat.

"I guess you're right. It's happened before," said the black hat.

"I'll drink to that," said the white hat. I was jolted and shocked. Are they talking about what I think they are talking about? Neither one of them said anything as the plane landed and we prepared to disembark. It then occurred to me where we were landing—not at Dallas/Ft. Worth. We were landing at Love Field, where President and Mrs. Kennedy landed on November 22, 1963. I've been studying the JFK assassination for many years and, like my parents, have never believed that Oswald acted alone. I walked past the oil men and tried not to stare, but I couldn't help wondering.

RUNNING ON EMPTY (2009)

I told myself that my third divorce would be my last, and I know it will be. I mean, who am I? Zsa Zsa Gabor? Elizabeth Taylor? Mickey Rooney? I remember reading about all their marriages and divorces in the *National Enquirer* that my mom used to buy at the IGA grocery store in Kenmore, Washington. Divorces always come with bankruptcies, hand in hand. I've had bankruptcies too. Not pleasant. Enough was enough. I needed stability. I'm now married to Ginger. She is my rock and my forever girl. She was a punk rocker and a cheerleader. How perfect and how cool is that? Ginger is exactly what I needed so I could flourish. Nothing against my ex-wives, I know that I was no picnic to be with, but I finally found the person that would keep me on the straight and narrow. I needed to grow and evolve, and I have.

I started running again after I met Ginger. My health improved, and I even dropped some weight. My friend Eric is also a runner, but he runs marathons. I couldn't do that. The farthest I've ever run is 10 kilometers, and that was in 1980 when I was 22 years old. I got to know Eric very well during 9/11. We were in Norfolk, Virginia, along with Theresa, another Citrus College professor. I had made contact with a retired admiral at a distance education showcase, and that led to Citrus College getting a contract with the Navy to deliver distance education courses to sailors around the world. We were at the Naval Base Norfolk to test the feasibility of our plan and discuss the details with the prime contractor, KEI Pearson. Of course, we were trapped back east after the 9/11 attacks and Eric, Theresa, and I formed a close bond that still exists today.

In 2009, Ginger and I were living in Azusa, California, in a light green rental house, the Green House, as Ginger called it. Behind our house were tiny one-bedroom apartments also owned by our landlord. The renters of those little rat-hole apartments were an unusual bunch living out sad mini-dramas. One of them I nicknamed the Underwear Man because he was always smoking outside in only his tighty whities.

He never spoke except one time when he asked Ginger for a match. There was a lady who liked to sunbathe topless and had a trucker boyfriend who showed up once a month. They would fight fiercely after an evening of hard drinking. One night I had to call the cops. He never came back. We also had tweakers who fidgeted, lit matches, dug holes in the lawn, drank Red Bulls that they threw on the ground, and preferred to jump the side-fence instead of walking around. Ginger and I worked hard, and my two young children, Leif and Caitlin, would come to stay every other week, according to the custody agreement. I continued to run and built up my endurance and strength.

One day, I had a powerful vision during my two-mile run up to Sierra Madre Avenue near the new housing development that lay between Azusa and Glendora. I had a vision of my friend Eric dying suddenly of a massive heart attack while he was running. It was a vivid and scary vision. I saw my dear friend suddenly stop running, twist around clutching his chest in agony, and collapse to the ground. There was nothing I could do. He was dead. After I had this frightening vision, I kept checking in on Eric to make sure he was okay. I'd call, drop by his office, and email him.

The years went by, and I faced one personal crisis after another. I kept running, even though I was mentally and physically exhausted. I lost my house in the divorce and bankruptcy. My credit was shot to hell, and my daughter was having a tough time in high school. Through all of it, Ginger was there, standing right next to me. Meanwhile, my friend Eric was a busy science dean, and our paths didn't cross that often. My impression was that he was doing okay, so I had all but forgotten about my vision.

In 2013, I heard that something tragic had happened on campus that impacted Eric. He was so distraught that he had to take nearly a year off from work. Eric was in the Citrus Library when a lady collapsed from a massive heart attack and died. He saw her suddenly stop walking, twist around clutching her chest in agony, and then collapse to the sidewalk in front of the library. There was nothing Eric could do. She was dead. Eric attempted CPR but was unsuccessful. My vision had come true, but it wasn't Eric, it was an old lady who died suddenly while visiting the campus with her daughter.

Before Eric was the science dean, he was a biology professor. Earlier in his academic career, he wanted to be a doctor. I think this old lady's death affected him in a myriad of ways. He developed post-traumatic stress from the incident. I spoke to Eric the few times I saw him on campus, but he wasn't doing well. The years went on, and finally, I had lunch with him at Legends, a 1950s style diner on Route 66 in Glendora. He told me about the incident and how it had changed his life. I told him about the vision I had of him dying of a heart attack in 2009. It seemed to be more than just coincidence. Eric said to me that he had spoken to his sister who is a psychic and she knew things about the lady who died that she couldn't have possibly known.

"An older lady in a blue sweater is contacting you," Eric's sister told him. His sister said that the lady was trying to reach out to Eric and comfort him and tell him that he did all he could and that it wasn't his fault. Even a doctor couldn't have saved her. This understanding developed from his sister's psychic session has helped Eric. He has moved on in his life and found greater peace.

I remember Jackson Browne's big hit in 1977, "Running on Empty." That was a pivotal year in my life. My first relationship was in trouble, and I was flunking out of the University of Washington. So many things that happened that year would happen again until I finally learned the lesson. You can't continue living your life without joy and fulfillment or commitment and discipline. I was having trouble balancing these things. As Jackson Browne sang so simply and poignantly:

I don't know how to tell you all just how crazy this life feels

Look around for the friends that I used to turn to, to pull me through

Looking into their eyes, I see them running too

Running on, running on empty

As odd as it sounds, the incident with the old lady dying in his arms helped Eric break up the logjam in his life. He is a better and happier person for the experience. I can say the same thing about me. All my negative experiences have made me a better and stronger man. Those events have brought me to the road I'm on now. They brought me to Ginger. I don't think Eric runs anymore, but I do. Slowly, methodically, and consistently, I run and will continue to run until it's no longer possible, and the tank is empty.

HARVEY RIDES! (2017)

I run, maybe jog is a better word, five or six times a week. Sometimes, I take a long walk instead. These runs and walks give me time to think, kind of like my own form of meditation. Some of my best ideas have come to me while running and walking. As a bonus, I figure that exercising allows me to eat the foods I like without fear of gaining too much weight. I don't want to wear tight clothes and when I gain weight my clothes are uncomfortably tight. My weight has fluctuated, since age 18, from 185 to 275 pounds. I don't have my father's metabolism. He remained trim up until the end, consistently around 175 pounds. I take more after my mother's side of the family where all the men are rather large. I guess there is no mystery, eat less, move more.

Like my father, Harvey Pekar, the celebrated author of *American Splendor*, kept his trim fighting weight throughout his life. In many ways, Harvey reminded me of my father, always in motion, smart, cantankerous, driven, gloomy, suspicious, and extremely thrifty. But at the same time, my father and Harvey could be generous and kind. Sadly, I never got to meet Harvey. He died in 2010. What I know about him I've learned from his comic books and graphic novels, and from Gary Dumm, his friend, and primary illustrator. I wish I could have met him; I think we could have been friends.

I wrote to Harvey's widow, Joyce Brabner, and even bought a few comic books and books from her that she graciously signed. I also purchased a Harvey doll from her. The somewhat frightening looking doll accompanied me in April 2016 when I traveled to Northern Norway with the director of my play *The Epiphany*. We were setting up and scouting for the production of the play that was to be performed in September 2016. I took photos of the Harvey doll in the snow and the trees surrounding our old farmhouse and sent them to Joyce. I did some research on Harvey and figured out where he used to live and where he would hang out in Cleveland, Ohio. I'd been to Cleveland before when I was pursuing my History doctorate at Bowling Green

State University, Bowling Green, Ohio, which was 125 miles West of Cleveland.

My decision to write a second edition to my anti-textbook, *Making History: A Personal Approach to Modern American History*, and to include comic book pages to the book, was inspired by Harvey Pekar. The first edition contained personal stories connected to the issues in each chapter, but I wanted more impact for the students. The problem was that I needed an illustrator to turn my autobiographical introductions from the book into comic book pages. I approached my friend Larry Jost, who is an excellent and talented illustrator, but he didn't have the time to take on another project. I then looked through old issues of *American Splendor* and noticed one artist whose style seemed to fit my vision. His style was very similar to that of my friend Larry. That artist was Gary Dumm. I wrote an email to Gary explaining my idea, and after sending him the manuscript to read, he agreed to illustrate *Making History*.

My wife Ginger and I visited Gary and his wife Laura in Cleveland in December 2016, and we talked about his initial work on the comic book pages. I stood and looked at Gary's artwork that lay on the same table and in the same room that was used when Gary worked with Harvey.

"Harvey probably wore out the wood flooring pacing around while we discussed the illustrations for *American Splendor*," said Gary. That was cool. We ate breakfast with Gary and Laura at a café in the Westside Market in Cleveland. It reminded me of the Pike Place Market in Seattle. The Westside Market had great food and was filled with so many unique sights and aromas. Ginger and I visited Harvey Pekar Park at the northwest corner of Coventry Road and Euclid Heights Boulevard in Cleveland Heights. That is where Harvey worked and lived while creating *American Splendor*. It was a fantastic trip, and we enjoyed meeting Gary and his talented wife, Laura. Harvey brought Gary and I together and now *Making History*, our anti-textbook, has been a big success and I believe that is mostly due to Gary's illustrations and Harvey's inspiration.

In May 2017, I was on one of my long walks around my neighborhood. I cover over two miles on these walks. Once a week I run this route, but on this one day, I was walking. Usually, I see bikers, serious bikers, riding on the streets where I run and walk. Sometimes they come in huge packs of 20–30 riders. They all wear those skin-tight spandex riding outfits that leave little to the imagination. They have little use for pedestrians, so you must be careful when you enter the crosswalk because they don't stop or slow down. I was on my way back having gone up the one-mile hill and back down when I spotted someone on an old bike who looked immediately out of place. I did a double-take because the man I saw looked just like Harvey Pekar. He dressed in very Harvey-like clothes and was riding slowly on a vintage bike, not like ones the speed racers use. He was by himself and seemed to be oblivious to everything around him and had an odd expression on his face like he was deep in thought and concerned about something. It gave me quite a jolt. No, could that be Harvey? I asked myself. It certainly looked like him, and the man seemed oddly anachronistic.

I usually see the same people every day when I run and walk. People develop routines. But I had never seen this man before and hadn't seen him since. I watched him for a few seconds, then checked my phone to see the time, looked up, and he was gone.

I decided that I would send an email to Gary Dumm and let him know that I had seen Harvey. I started my inquiry more abstractly and entitled the email: Weird Question.

"Did Harvey ever ride a bicycle?" I asked.

"That is a weird question! Except for Harvey's doing push-ups on David Letterman, I never saw him do any exercise…but he did pace around our dining room table like a maniac, talking. So, to answer your original question, I'd guess that he hadn't ridden a bicycle since he was a kid." I thought more about this incident and its meaning. Gary sent me a follow-up email.

"Well, you know, somewhere in the multiverse Harvey rides, and perhaps you were privileged to see that version of our world with him thinking and riding and probably humming some Bebop!" That made me happy. I'm convinced that the man I saw was Harvey Pekar, or more properly, a ghost image of Harvey. He was other-worldly in his appearance and oblivious to me and everything else around him. I remember seeing a photo of his gravestone. The epitaph has a quote from Harvey:

"Life is about women, gigs, and bein' creative." In the life beyond this one, Harvey rides.

COSMOPOLITAN

I enjoy traveling and learning about different people, their culture, their food, their folklore, and the way they live. Often, I adopt some of the aspects of those cultures and make them my own. I've read that the Vikings would conquer foreign lands and then stay only to assimilate quickly into the customs and culture of their victims leaving only Norse place names as a reminder of what had happened. That is why you find city names in the United Kingdom like Scarborough, Rawcliffe, Ravenfield, Knutsford, Ormskirk, Holdenby, Formby, and Coleby, among many others. To be cosmopolitan is to be familiar with and at ease in many different countries and cultures.

American humorist Will Rogers once said that he never met a man he didn't like. Well, I can honestly say that I've never met a culture I didn't like. Not surprisingly, Spock was my favorite character on the original *Star Trek* TV series. In an episode called "Is There in Truth, No Beauty?" Spock wore an Infinite Diversity Through Infinite Combinations (IDIC) pin on his uniform. The dialogue revealed that this ethos was at the foundation of his Vulcan culture. Spock went on to say, "The glory of creation is in its infinite diversity. And the ways our differences combine to create meaning and beauty."

Although I admire the diversity of cultures on our planet, I also recognize how alike we all are. As John F. Kennedy said in a commencement speech, June 10, 1963, just a little over five months before his assassination:

So, let us not be blind to our differences—but let us also direct attention to our common interests and to the means by which those differences can be resolved. And if we cannot end now our differences, at least we can help make the world safe for diversity. For, in the final analysis, our most basic common link is that we all inhabit this small planet. We all breathe the same air. We all cherish our children's future. And we are all mortal.

One of the things that unites all cultures on Earth is the paranormal. Every culture has ghost stories. My interest in the paranormal often drives my choice of travel destination, or at least it's some aspect of the choice.

On September 2, 2017, my wife Ginger, me, my mother-in-law Mary, and my sister-in-law Courtney, were all visiting San Diego, California. It was a Labor Day weekend and my birthday celebration (September 3). We had planned to attend the Plumeria Festival at Balboa Park, tour the USS Midway, and I insisted on a ghost tour. Michael was the ghost tour guide with San Diego Ghost Tours. We met at the Fountain in front of Fiesta De Reyes in Old Town San Diego State Historic Park at 9 pm. There were probably a dozen other people in our tour group. We started our walking tour through the courtyard, and the exceedingly earnest and serious Michael told us about the ghosts he had seen in and around the buildings there. We proceeded to the Whaley House that is well known for its hauntings. Michael, who never smiled even once, said that remodeling had reduced the presence of spirits in the house. Our next stop was the El Campo Santo Cemetery established in 1849. There are 477 people buried in the cemetery, but not all of them within the current walls of the graveyard. Some of the graves are now under the sidewalk and the street. Brass discs inscribed "Grave Site" marked those poor souls' final resting places. Close by was what Michael described as the vortex. He produced an EMF (electromagnetic field) meter from his jacket pocket and started to take readings. He said the vortex hovered near that spot where we stood. Everyone was encouraged to feel the vortex. I didn't feel anything.

As we continued our ghost tour, we were coming up to what would be the pièce de résistance of the tour. Michael had special permission to tour the Cosmopolitan Hotel, the most haunted location in San Diego. Our guide set us up in the bar and poured us all some water in glasses from behind the bar. He lectured on the history of the hotel. Between 1827 and 1829, Don Juan Bandini had an adobe home built on the site where the hotel is now. Bandini was typical of most Mexican Californio people of his time. Cattle ranching made him rich. He held various public offices and was influential throughout Southern

California. His three daughters were said to be the most beautiful women in California—Josefa, Arcadia, and Ysidora. The youngest, Ysidora, fell from the roof of their home and died. According to legend, it's her ghost that haunts room 11 in the hotel.

After the Mexican-American War of 1848, Don Juan Bandini lost his wealth, like so many other Mexican Californios, and had to sell his home. In 1869, American stagecoach operator Albert Seeley, and his wife Emily bought the house for $2,000 in gold and made the home into a stagecoach stop and hotel. When the railroads came, Seeley's stagecoach operation became obsolete, and the cultural center of San Diego shifted from Old Town to New Town (the Gaslamp Quarter of today's downtown). Seeley sold the building in 1888.

In the 21st century, the Cosmopolitan Hotel has returned to its former glory thanks to a multi-million-dollar restoration project. In the spirit of the 1870s, one can see historical reproduction furnishings, original floorboards, wainscoting, windows, window and door frames, and in one room you can still see some of Don Juan's original adobe.

As Michael lectured, I felt something on the back of my neck, the hairs standing on end, and a chill. I turned around and noticed the staircase behind me. I investigated. I stood by the staircase by a portrait on the wall. As I stood there, I felt a hand lightly brush up against my left arm. It was cold, gentle, but definite. It felt feminine. I turned around to look at the painting on the wall. The portrait was of Albert and Emily Seeley. I believe it was the ghost of Emily Seeley who had touched me. I told Michael, and he wasn't surprised.

Next, he had us sit down around the dining room table adjacent to the bar. He said that the ghosts all visit in that room and that he could see them because he was experienced and in tune with the spirits. He had us all try to feel them, some of our group said they felt something, most didn't. Some didn't even dare to enter the dining room. I didn't feel or see anything. As we moved back out to the bar, Courtney yelled out. Ginger investigated and discovered a bristle stuck in her arm. We removed it, and she was okay. I believe it was a bristle from an old brush. Michael said that Ysidora, the daughter of Don Juan Bandini who fell to her death, loved to brush her hair and loves to touch the hair of visitors. Who knows, maybe the bristle that embedded itself mysteriously in Courtney's arm came from the brush of Ysidora's ghost.

The Travel Channel series, *Ghost Adventures*, visited the Cosmopolitan Hotel. They discovered that rooms four and five, where Don Juan Bandini and his wife lived, were haunted. They believe that there is a residual haunting, an intelligent haunting, and objects that are haunted in the hotel. A residual haunting is like a tape loop that plays over and over. An intelligent haunting interacts with living people. It has been reported that the rocking chair and bed that belonged to Ysidora are haunted. The rocking chair moves on its own. There is also a ghost man named Carlos who is dressed like an old cowboy and plays guitar and sings.

I didn't see any self-propelled rockers or singing cowboy ghosts; I only felt a woman's ghostly hand brush against my arm, that was real and enough for me to be convinced that the Cosmopolitan Hotel is indeed haunted. I suppose, when you think about it, the dead have their own culture that we don't fully understand. I've caught glimpses of the culture of the dead and felt its presence over the years, but it's still not entirely known to us who live in the culture of the living. I suppose we'll all find out someday when our mortality in this world catches up to us and we travel to the other side and assimilate into the Great Unknown as timeless entities.

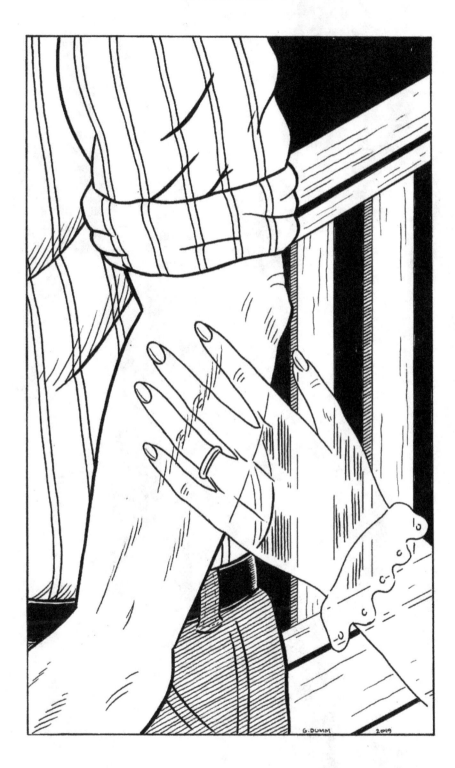

SAND PITS (2018)

In April 2018, I was dreaming of the old sand pits above the house where I grew up in Kenmore, Washington. The sand pits were just below the old Nike missile site, which was to the north. There was also a reservoir that had been built in 1962 just above the sand pits and south of the Nike site that was eventually decommissioned in 1964. All the kids that I knew loved the sand pits because you could be wild and free. It was a perfect place to conduct mischief. There were madrona trees on the outer edge where we would seek shade on hot days.

Madrona trees are native to the Pacific Northwest, and their berries were used by Indians as food, mainly to make a cider type drink. They used the bark and leaves for medicinal purposes. Madrona trees are evergreens with dark green leaves. The unique thing about madrona trees is their bark. These mysterious trees lose their rusty red papery bark in summer. The bark peels off to reveal a bare trunk with a greenish, silvery satin sheen. Some have described this bald trunk as being a pistachio color. The flowers of the madrona that blossom in spring smell like subtle lilacs.

Long before white settlement in the Puget Sound, the Hachuahbsh (meaning people of a large lake) inhabited the area. They later became part of the Duwamish tribe. I always assumed that Indians used the sand pit area for some religious reason. Indians never burned the wood of a madrona because they thought of the tree as sacred. The Indian legend about the madrona is fascinating. A young Indian man had an illegitimate love affair. Because of this indiscretion, his skin peeled off in shame as he transformed into the first madrona tree, From the sand pits, you could see down to Lake Washington (the large lake). It was a special magical place.

One day, in the summer of 1970, I decided that I was going to make a firebomb. I found a cylindrical shipping container, lined it with plastic, and filled it with gasoline. I surrounded the container with ten cherry bombs that my brother got from the Tulalip Indian reservation when he was home on leave from the Vietnam War. I tied the fuses together with a longer fuse. I strapped the incendiary bomb to the rack on the back of my bike and headed up to the sand pits. When I got there, I noticed that no one was around—that was good because this was going to be risky. Some newer houses had been built just across the street about 100 yards away, so I had to make sure no one was watching me. I placed the firebomb in the middle of the sand pits, then, I lit the fuse and ran to seek cover behind the stand of madrona trees. It took longer than I expected before it blew. And boy did it blow. The explosion was so loud that it shook the windows of the houses on the other side of the street. The fireball went 30 to 40 feet into the air and even singed some of the leaves high up in the madrona trees. I was knocked back on my butt by the blast. The smell of gunpowder and gasoline filled the air and thick black smoke issued from the large hole where the incendiary bomb had been. I was frightened and especially so when people came running out of their houses in full panic to see what had happened. I jumped on my bike and raced down the hill and back home. Luckily, no one was hurt, and I survived and didn't get in trouble. I never returned to the sand pits for fear of being discovered as the mad fire bomber who terrorized that quiet hilltop neighborhood on a lazy summer day in 1970.

Back to the dream. I was in the sand pits again, at the scene of the crime. It was a sunny day, and the wind was blowing gently and rustling the leaves of the majestic madrona trees. On the road where the houses had been, there was now a factory. I'm not sure what type of factory but it seemed to be related to the production of military equipment. I sat at the base of a giant madrona and took in the beautiful day. Suddenly, at the entrance of the factory at the top of the road on the hill by the sand pits, there was trouble. Several men were arguing loudly, some of them in uniforms. The arguments grew even louder, and a few of the men began to grapple and were pushing each other. A few of them drew out their pistols, and one man in uniform had a rifle. The rifleman shot the others, and then he looked at me. I knew I was in trouble because he stared straight at me and aimed his rifle. As I stood up to run, I noticed two little boys standing next to me. They were innocently playing in the sand. I grabbed them and ran down the hill to safety. Gunshots rang out, and the rounds hit the pavement around us, zing, zing, zing! We sought cover behind a concrete wall by a house, and the two little boys and I were safe, at least temporarily. It was then that I woke up from this terrifying dream.

My heart was pounding, and I was breathing heavily when I woke up from this nightmare. I looked around the bedroom, and I could see dark human shadows moving around on the ceiling and the walls. My wife Ginger wasn't in bed; she was working in her workshop still. The dark shapes swirled around me, elongated and menacing. I closed my eyes and said: "I believe in God and you aren't welcome here. We're protected in this house, Jesus help me. Get out!" The dark shadowy humanoid entities disappeared. It took me several minutes to calm down. Why had this happened and what were these dark shadowy things? I guess that it had something to do with the sand pits and the firebombing. Maybe I had not only disturbed the neighbors nearby the sand pits, but I had awakened some spirits that resided in that sacred spot by the madrona trees and I had caused the sacred trees to be slightly burned. I figured this haunting was a punishment for my crime and the dark shadows were there to remind me. Be careful dear readers. As my friend Gene told me after his death, "What we do in this life echoes in all of eternity."

VALLEY CENTER (2018)

Recently, I've decided to take long walks, more than four miles, instead of running two miles. Walking is easier on my nearly 60-year-old joints and it also gives me more time to think. I like the idea of meditation, but I find it very difficult to sit in one position. I've discovered that I can achieve a meditative state while walking. On these walks, I can think clearly and relax. Sometimes I listen to audiobooks or music, but lately I walk with my headphones on just to cancel out some of the noise around me. When I do, I begin to only pay attention to my breathing and my methodical footsteps. I call this walking meditation.

There is one particular stretch of my daily walk where I seem to be able to achieve this meditative state most easily and also make some remarkable paranormal connections. The ability to communicate with the dead is known as theurgy or mediumship. My walking meditation route takes me up a road called Valley Center Avenue in Glendora, California. The road heads north toward a valley by Glendora Mountain Road. There is a wash that follows along Valley Center. The magical stretch of road is approximately three-quarters of a mile long and inclined moderately. Although cars drive by, it doesn't distract me because I have my headphones. I often record myself with my phone as I have my spiritual connections.

Not surprisingly, the Freemasons built their lodge at the beginning of this stretch of road in 1963. I think they chose their location to enhance their ritual magic practices. Shoshone artifacts dating back to 6000 BC have been found in Glendora. I believe Valley Center was a medicine road for the Shoshone who lived here first. From the spiritual connections I've made on my walks up Valley Center, I've encountered Native Americans, citrus growers, cowboys, settlers, Spaniards, Mexicans, and others. I've also talked with friends and have taken a few requests from friends and loved ones to contact their relatives.

When I open up all hailing frequencies (an homage to Lieutenant Uhura from the original *Star Trek* TV series), many spirits line up to speak to me, sometimes all at once until I call out one of them. When I establish a relaxed focus and receive their communications, I usually see a faint image of the person, or hear their voice, or sometimes it appears as handwriting (often golden) that I can see. Some of these spirits are speaking in a language I don't understand (Spanish or a native language), other times they speak in English. They are intelligent, not residual spirits, because they can answer my questions.

In the end of May 2018, I took such a walk and began to have a vision. I saw my friend Gene Thorkildsen again. I wanted to ask him more questions and find out what he meant by "it's all true."

"What you think is true, is true." He said.

"What I think?" I asked.

"Yes," he said.

"So, all paranormal stuff is true?"

"Yes."

"Magic is real?"

"Yes."

"Am I some kind of prophet or messenger?"
"Yes, that's why you're writing these books. Big responsibility."

"Everything I suspect to be true, it's true?"

"Yes, except for silly things."

"Okay, you mean like Elvis living in Miami Beach?" Gene just smiled.

"How do I convince people? There are lots of skeptics."

"Provide examples, persistence, support the scientists, and you won't be able to convince hardcore skeptics, so don't waste your time."

"Right," I said. Gene was starting to fade away as my concentration began to give way to traffic noise and other distractions. Then I thought about my most recent play that deals with the danger posed by Russia to Europe and specifically to Norway.

"Am I right about the threat to Norway from Russia?" "Yes. Produce the play now!" he said. Great, now I feel an even bigger responsibility than I did before. I drifted back to our original conversation.

"Why no shoes?" I asked.

"We fly and float. There's no need for shoes, I always liked being barefoot anyway."

"Cool." He was fading again. I knew my time with him was limited. As I continued my walk, I thought deeply about the source, the divine or God, what I've been reading about, the third level of consciousness. "Is there God?" I asked.

"You already know, your mom told you," he said as his voice grew more distant and his image continued to fade and seemed intermittent. "It is all."

"God is all?"

"Yes. And it is nothing," he added. He was barely audible or visible.

"What about aliens…are they here, you know, visiting us?"

"We are the aliens," said Gene. I was in shock from all this information and clarification. I thought about how lucky I was to be able to have contact with my friend.

"I know it's hard for you to communicate, I'll let you go," I said.

"Yes, it's hard." Then, he was gone.

I still have more questions, but I also feel like maybe it's greedy of me to take up so much of his energy and time, well, I guess time doesn't matter, as he told me before, but energy for sure. Maybe I should not try to talk to him anymore and just allow only his family to contact him. He has done enough for me, both in his life, and now in the afterlife.

On one of my contemplative walks in early June 2018, I had a communication with my friend and colleague Maia. She died nearly two years ago. I'll share the dialogue I had with her. I saw a faint image of Maia and heard a faint voice and was able to see and read her responses in the form of handwriting.

"How are you, my friend?" I asked.

"Fine," she said.

"Are you okay? Where are you?" I asked.

"I'm home."

"Home?"

"Yes."

I thought for a moment because I knew she was from Idaho and was living in Idaho when she passed away.

"Oh, like your own planet Idaho?" I asked.

She laughed. "Yes, very funny," she said.

"Will you visit our paranormal class and give us a sign of your presence?" I asked.

"Yes."

That was a quick answer, I thought. *Cool.* I decided to dig deeper as I continued walking up Valley Center on the lookout for passersby who might think I was delusional. "Is there God? I asked.

She waited for a while before answering. "Yes, many."

"Many? What do you mean?"

"Yes, each of us," she said.

Sometimes these communications get unclear, with interference, like psychic static. I wanted to make sure I understood her. "Oh, I see, a part of God in each of us?" I asked.

"Yes."

I wanted to check something that my friend Gene told me about time. "Time?" I asked.

"It's all one, no difference," she said.

I could tell this was exhausting for her and more people were approaching on Valley Center, so I knew I didn't have much more time to talk to Maia. "You're a good person and you have angel hair," I said.

She smiled. "Thank you. You're a good person," she said.

That was a nice boost of confidence, so I went further. "Will my *Timeless* books be successful?

"Yes, very much, bestsellers," she said.

We shall see dear readers, that is very much up to you.

A week later, on another meditative walk, I spoke with Maia again, from the great beyond. I asked more specific questions about her existence beyond death. She told me she is living as herself in another dimension but is also communicating with me in the spiritual dimension at the same time. This is something I may also be doing after having experienced some forks in the road of time or Alternate Life Experiences (ALE) as I also call them.

"What do you think of my nine lives idea?" I asked.

"I'm not sure if it's limited to nine," she said, "but there is reincarnation," she added.

"Is it like, I think that at one point...do you stop being reincarnated as yourself, continuing on without a break really, in progression in your life? Do we do this until we reach old age and then get reincarnated? Is that what happens?" I asked.

"Those are transitions before reincarnation," she said.

"Okay," I said. "The reason I ask is because my sister is…I saw her as a young girl…I think she's a young girl now, living her life again, so could that be possible too, to go back in time to a younger age?

"It's one possibility," she said. "You go back to where you wanted to go back to or you continue on where you are at."

"Is it up to you? Do you choose, or…?"

"Yes," she said.

I had to think this through.

"So, in other words, there are these forks in the road of time where we die in one dimension and live on in another, either directly, without skipping a beat, the same age and everything as if death never happened. Or, you can go back in time, or you can go forward in time I suppose. And at a certain point you reach old age and you die and then you get reincarnated. Is that true?"

"Yes," she said.

"Now I think I understand." I tried to draw out my idea and illustrate this ALE process. Please see the illustration on the next page.

"Do all the paths have one spiritual component?" I asked. "All, of the alternate you? Just one spiritual you?

"There is the one," she said. "All the different parts of you share the one spiritual you. The spiritual you goes with you after you die of old age into your new identity."

"Complicated," I said.

"Don't be afraid of complexity," said Maia.

"I know, I'm just trying to figure it out. How many of *you* are there?"

"Twenty-seven," she said.

"That seems like a lot."

"I know."

"How many of *me* are there?" I asked.

"Ahh, four or five, maybe more. Not sure," she said.

"You're going to be in the next book," I said.

"Cool."

I had to stop for a minute as someone walked by. Then I resumed my conversation with Maia.

OUR PERSONAL QUANTUM REALITY

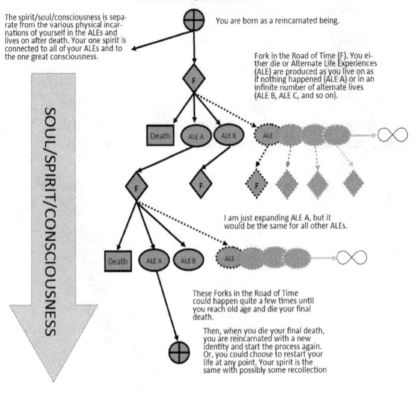

The spirit/soul/consciousness is separate from the various physical incarnations of yourself in the ALEs and lives on after death. Your one spirit is connected to all of your ALEs and to the one great consciousness.

You are born as a reincarnated being.

Fork in the Road of Time (F). You either die or Alternate Life Experiences (ALE) are produced as you live on as if nothing happened (ALE A) or in an infinite number of alternate lives (ALE B, ALE C, and so on).

SOUL/SPIRIT/CONSCIOUSNESS

Death   ALE A   ALE B   ALE   ∞

I am just expanding ALE A, but it would be the same for all other ALEs.

Death   ALE A   ALE B   ALE   ∞

These Forks in the Road of Time could happen quite a few times until you reach old age and die your final death.

Then, when you die your final death, you are reincarnated with a new identity and start the process again. Or, you could choose to restart your life at any point. Your spirit is the same with possibly some recollection

I base this theory on quantum mechanics and in particular quantum superposition. We exist as both particles and waves (particle-wave duality). The world we see is the particle form of matter. However, we are, in the quantum sense, wave forms and probabilities in motion. We are timeless. Consciousness is funda-

mental and creates everything in the multiverse. Our worlds are constructed when we observe everything around us and we shape our own realities. I believe that the ALE can also go back in time so you can relive a portion of your life or forward in time. Consider the illustrations above and to the left. When I take my morning walk I'm really all of these men in different phases and different locations on my walk. I am movement and a waveform in motion. When someone observes me, they see a man, a physical particle being. In quantum reality, I'm a wave in motion. If you speed me up, I am just a blur, or a streak, like the flash or a wave.

"Wanted to ask you about the one. The spiritual you, the ALEs…so they all share the same spiritual you," I asked. There was no answer. Maybe she was tired, or the connection was lost.

"I need to understand more about that. What does it mean? Is there just one consciousness for all of us, like the Buddhists say?" I asked.

"Yes."

"Our spiritual one is part of that one?"

"Yes."

"It's difficult, but I'll keep pushing on…I'll eventually understand," I said.

"The ONE. There is a spiritual us that is born and then all the subsequent physical incarnations. There is no other," she said.

"Wait. What does that mean?" I asked.

"The spiritual one of us is part of the spiritual whole," she said.

People were approaching so I had to hurry. "Is consciousness fundamental, like Dean Radin says?" I asked.

"Yes, how else do you think I could be talking to you," she said. We both laughed.

"What about bigfoot? Your friend anthropology professor Grover Krantz at Washington State University, he studied the Sasquatch. I had an experience, never got to talk to you about it."

"I'm open to it, not sure, but maybe. I liked Grover." And then she faded away.

All this information that I've obtained from Maia and Gene has helped me. I believe that we're timeless, and get many chances, many lives. I also believe that you have a choice in old age when you pass from this world. I think you will be able to choose whether you want to be reincarnated as a different person with a new identity or go back in time as yourself. How wonderful. In my reading of quantum mechanics and how the sub-atomic world operates, I've learned that a history or backstory is developed by the process of quantum observation. Scaled up to our macro-world, I believe this is also true for the ALE. Therefore, in your physical existence, you may not be aware that you have lived another physical existence prior to the fork in the road of time.

Our fear of death is unwarranted. Some of us are so afraid of death that we don't truly live. Those that have passed on can help us to understand. I want to make a difference. I've decided to help people contact their dead relatives, but I was unsure about taking money for the service. I asked different people, including psychic mediums, and they convinced me that if you're providing a unique service that is meaningful and helpful to people, then there is nothing wrong with receiving fair compensation. That made sense to me. Of course, I'd also like them to buy my *Timeless* books. I have this gift of mediumship for a reason. The books, the psychic mediumship, the paranormal college course, and my monthly radio show, and my eventual TV show are all part of the way in which I deliver the spiritual message. I need to do this. It's my calling. So, I'll keep walking up Valley Center, the Big Medicine Road, writing my books, teaching my course, and producing my radio show and working on my TV show, and maybe someday I can help you my dear readers. I hope that day is today.

RED LIGHT (2018)

Have you ever been in a terrifyingly dangerous situation where time seemed to slow down? Some scientists call this slow-motion perception, and it's an area of study that has produced conflicting theories. In the movie *The Matrix*, characters could get out of the way of bullets because they could slow down time while battling each other. Is this kind of a time warp possible?

I had a terrifying experience while I was in the US Army helicopter flight school in 1983 at Fort Rucker, Alabama. Everything was going well in the Korean War vintage TH-55 two-seat helicopter. I was enjoying my solo flight in a clear blue Alabama sky by myself. As I made my approach to the stage field, my anti-torque pedals became stuck. I couldn't move them. Anti-torque pedals control the yaw or the direction you are pointing in as you fly. The tail rotor provides anti-torque for the main rotor and the pedals control the tail rotor. If I couldn't get the pedals unstuck, I would begin to spin uncontrollably and crash. I was coming closer to the runway and the pedals were impossible to move, they were frozen stuck. The helicopter began to spin. Red warning lights flashed on, but I remained calm as everything slowed down. In this slow-motion time warp, I felt certain that everything would be okay, and I felt warm and safe. I was able to carefully manipulate the pedals to unstick them and I landed safely avoiding a certain crash and possible death.

Three years ago, I was driving through Los Angeles on the 105 freeway with my wife Ginger and my son Byron. We were going to drop off Byron at Los Angeles International Airport (LAX). We were chatting and laughing and having a good time. Then, a truck on my right began to come into our lane. At the same time, a car on the left was also making its way into my lane. If that wasn't bad enough, the car directly in front of me slammed on the brakes. All I could see were red brake lights and all I could hear was the horrible screeching of tires on the pavement surrounding us. We were about to be sandwiched in between two vehicles as we rear-ended another one in front of us at a high rate of speed. Behind me was another big truck. It was a seemingly no-win situation with possible deadly consequences. Time then slowed down. I felt like I had all the time in the world to react and figure out a solution. I once again felt a warm presence and was filled with confidence and equanimity. I braked and slowed down just enough to sneak in behind the car on my left and avoided an accident. It was a miracle. Ginger asked me how I did it. My son told me what a great emergency driver I was, but it wasn't just me, I had help.

On June 29, 2018, I was driving on Arrow Highway in Glendora, California, with my youngest son. It was a bright, sunny day and all seemed right with the world. I was in no way expecting something terrible to happen. We were looking for an address as I approached a traffic light at the intersection of Arrow Highway and Sunflower. One second the light was green, the next second it was red. I was barreling through the middle of the intersection as a car on the left accelerated from the south toward us, and a car on the right approached from the north. We were about to be struck broadside by both cars when time slowed down. I was able to swerve and maneuver between the two cars like I was threading the eye of a needle with inches to spare. How could I have done that? I see it as a miracle that I could act so quickly. I believe it was yet another fork in the road of time. The other two incidents were also forks in the road of time. How can all this be explained?

Some scientists believe that the brain and perception speed up because of the massive influx of adrenaline during a dangerous incident. Others contend that it's only an illusion. Researcher David Eagleman concluded that time doesn't slow down during a life-threatening event, instead, retrospectively, people's memories are more densely packed, and the event only seems to be slowed down. Still more scientists hold that the perception of time can slow down because the brain works more quickly when a person is in danger. With the outside world seeming to move more slowly, a person can respond to the threat faster than usual. This rapid response is a survival mechanism. Is it merely that external events slow down relative to the speedy brain function and time itself is not affected and there is nothing paranormal about this phenomenon? But how does this work exactly?

Most scientists believe that time doesn't slow down. Some attribute this effect to what they call increased memory packing. The adrenaline rush while a person is in a dangerous situation caused your perception of sights, sounds, smells, and touch to be more densely packed into memory. This densely packed memory of the event seems to be different than normal memory (either before and after the incident) and gives a person the illusion of time slowing down. Other scientists believe that the perceived warping of time doesn't result from the adrenaline rush while in danger, instead, it's an illusion.

Scientists at the Baylor College of Medicine set up an experiment having volunteers dive backward from a great height into a safety net. The test subjects would reach a speed of 70 miles per hour in their 150-foot drop to the net. Those who were tested reported that their own falls lasted one-third longer than the ones they observed of others. The scientists even gave the participants special wristwatches that flashed numbers at a high rate of speed. They wanted to see if test subjects could read those numbers while falling, thereby testing the theory of whether or not they could slow down time. The participants could not read the flickering set of numbers, so scientists concluded that the time slowing down phenomena was an illusion.

The problem with these experiments and with the accompanying explanations is that they are looking at this phenomenon from the standpoint of classical physics and not quantum physics. These experiments utilize the classic arrow of time that is straight, goes only in one direction and is constant in terms of speed. However, Albert Einstein's famous theory of relativity showed that as a person traveling through space approaches the speed of light, time does slow down for the traveler relative to the observer back on Earth. Could it be that the dangerous situation opens up a quantum entangled time warp momentarily? I believe so, and a quantum explanation is needed. The person in danger enters into a quantum state where all matter, from the subatomic to the macro world we usually see, is connected through what is called quantum entanglement. This connection allows instantaneous effects across all dimensions of time and space. In that quantum state, the person in danger is no longer experiencing the normal space-time they encounter under non-life-threatening situations. Therefore, time does slow down for them relative to the observer.

Double-slit experiments have shown that atoms and light act as waves when not observed and particles when observed. This observation effect is normally referred to as the quantum enigma. In other words, the observer creates their own reality. In extreme danger, we break from that normal day to day reality and enter into the quantum entanglement. There are other examples of quantum effects in the macro world. Baseball players have explained that when they are in the zone, they can see the baseball better and hit it more successfully. They say the ball slows down for them. Soldiers in combat have noted a similar slow down as they are under fire.

So, is the phenomenon of time slowing down a memory trick? Is it memory packing caused by an adrenaline rush? Could it be only an illusion? Or is it something else entirely? There are other instances where people have reported time being slowed down or sped up. Does time fly while you're having fun? Does the clock move more slowly when you look at it? Do we have trouble telling time passing while we're tired? Does suppressing one's emotions slow down time? Do altered states of consciousness (through meditation, drugs, etc.) effect time? Does increased temperature speed up time? Does time fly by when you get older? Does everyone have their own natural tempo and perception of time? All of these would be interesting lines of inquiry.

In my case, I believe the crisis point where I ran the red light opened a time warp where I was able to remove my son and me from danger in one dimension. I shudder to think what happened in the other dimensions or as I call them Alternate Life Experiences (ALEs). In this ALE we're okay, and the other cars and occupants are unharmed. In the other ALEs, it could have been catastrophic for all parties. This latest red-light incident was similar to the other forks in the road of time that

I mentioned earlier, and I've collected quite a few of them now. I also believe that my guardian angel Theodora, who is also my spirit guide along with Ozzie the Warrior, had a hand in keeping us safe because I felt a warm presence and complete calm and belief that everything was going to be okay. This incident reminded me of how fast things can go wrong with absolutely no warning. Even a momentary distraction can prove to be disastrous or maybe the traffic lights malfunctioned. Luckily, my son and I are okay, in this dimension. Although I do believe that we're all timeless, I can't be reckless with the life I have now. How many forks in the road will I have? Is it an infinite number? If it's a finite number and I exceed that, what would happen? No one knows.

I'm reminded of what my dear friends Gene and Maia told me:

"You are the ghosts in our world." I think I understand now. We're all ghosts. Red lights and red flags are there for a reason and we must heed the warning they give. Until we figure out all this quantum entanglement, I would suggest, dear readers, to pay attention, and remember what we all learned in kindergarten: red light means stop, and green light means go. I wish you all to have nothing but a wave of green lights but be careful out there.

ANZAR'S ANSWERS (2018-2019)

In 1997, I had an encounter with an alien primordial mystic named the Progenitor. Nearly 21 years later, I felt I was ready to contact him again. In November 2018 during one of my meditative walks, I asked my spirit guides to connect me with the Progenitor. I had read that some of us here on Earth are related to ancient aliens. I always suspected that I was different, but was I *that* different? I have read and heard that some alien races were friendly, and some were not.

"You said you were the original mystic. Am I related to you?" I asked.

"Yes," he said, in a slightly husky voice inside my head. I didn't see his face as I did in 1997, but I could hear his voice.

"So, we're some sort of hybrids?" I asked.

"Yes."

"What alien race are we?" He said something that I didn't understand, it sounded like he said Assyrians, but then he continued.

"Arcturians." What are Arcturians? I thought to myself; I would have to do more research.

"Am I doing the right things to help people? Any advice or wisdom?" I asked.

"Follow the hand that points to love, redemption, then the world is saved, and we all stand protected," he said. The communication ended abruptly, and I was in shock. Oh my God, am I an alien? But then I remembered that a few months before, my friend Gene told me that *we* are the aliens. It was all starting to make sense.

I spoke to the Progenitor again a week later and was better prepared with my questions.

"Were you the original alien contact for our planet?" I asked.

"Yes," he said.

"You helped early man become who we are today?"

"Yes."

"What's your name?"

"Anzar."

"Where do you come from?"

"Orion, Rigel."

"Okay," I said. I began to think even more deeply. Why was I having this contact now? Why did I write the first *Timeless* book? I got the feeling that I was caught up in something much larger than myself.

"Is something about to happen?" I asked.

"All is about to be revealed, stand ready, on guard, stick to the truth, trust your friends, and family. In anxious times people seek the comfort of those who are calm and rational, it is reassuring. It will be revealed soon…the contact that has been going on." Wow. I wondered if that would be a good thing or a bad thing? I felt privileged to be getting the information.

My friend Terry Lovelace, who had himself been abducted, researched the name Anzar and came up with some interesting details. In the language of the Basque people of Northeastern Spain, bordering France, Anzar means "lives near a pasture." Basques are a unique and old culture perhaps tied to Neolithic man. In my research, I found that in the Amazigh (or Berber) culture of North Africa, Anzar is the god of rain. There is a school named Anzar High School in the central Californian city of San Juan Bautista. The city was named after the mission of the same name and founded by Fermín de Francisco Lasuén de Arasqueta who was a Basque Franciscan missionary. He helped found eight other California missions.

The name Anzar is also a common one in the Muslim world. There is a town named Anzar in Northern Iran populated by the Azeris. Anzar, and its various spellings (i.e., Anzer, Ansar), means pure gold, angel of paradise, self-assurance, independence, and self-confidence, in Arabic. In the year 711, the Islamic Moors from northern Africa invaded Spain. The Moors went on to occupy Sicily as well. Five-hundred years later the Moors were defeated and driven out of Sicily and with the Fall of Granada in 1492, Muslim rule of Spain ended.

There is a hypothesis that Rh-negative blood has alien origins. Everybody on Earth has either O, A, B, or AB type blood. Your blood is also classified as either Rh-positive or Rh-negative. The Rhesus factor (based on lineage to Rhesus monkeys) refers to a specific antigen in the blood. Some 85 percent of the world's population carry the antigen and are Rh positive. The remaining 15 percent don't carry the antigen and have Rh negative blood. If man and ape had evolved from the same ancestor, their blood would have the same Rh factor. All primates on Earth have Rh-positive blood. So where did this Rh-negative blood come from? Most scientists say that is a simple mutation. Others say that it is of alien origin.

The International Community for Alien Research (ICAR) compiled information from over 53,000 people who have had alien contact. The chart below shows the percentage of people for each blood type, worldwide, and the corresponding percentage of that blood type that have been contacted by extra-terrestrials.

Blood Type	Percent of Total Population	Percent of Abductees
O neg	7	36
O pos	37	27
A pos	36	13
AB neg	1	10
A neg	6	5
B pos	9	3
AB pos	3	3
B neg	1	3

We can see from this data that aliens prefer type O blood and especially O negative. Scientists say that Rh-negative blood types developed only 25,000 to 40,000 years ago. O negative is also the universal donor but can only receive their own blood. Rh-negative men and women tend to have a sixth vertebrae, a lower body temperature, and lower than normal blood pressure. To tie this all up we know that the Basques have the highest percentage of Rh-negative blood in the world, over 30 percent. This blood type data may be a connection to Anzar and our possible alien origins.

I spoke to Anzar again in early December 2018. I was beginning to feel a sense of urgency in my mission to help people understand and not fear the paranormal.

"What else should I be doing?" I asked.

"Keep going. Be aware. Stay on the path. Realize how unique you are. Focus your energy and your determination. Train others for the future. You will know who is on the side of the light and who isn't," he said. Although the communication with the primordial mystic progenitor is enlightening and very cool, it also makes me think about who else may be getting this information? Am I the only one?

On the first day of Winter, December 21, 2018, I asked Anzar for advice.

"Caution. Proceed with caution. Help people understand and prepare. It will be audible when it happens, the big reveal. Visual will come later," he said.

"Audible from who? Our leaders?"

"Yes."

"Who?" I asked. He didn't answer.

"You are the Consciousness, be one with the Consciousness, rise to the highest level of your expectations and then exceed them. There is no boundary, no limit, except for those that are self-imposed or imposed by others, which you can ignore," he said.

"How are we related again? What race are we?"

"Arcturian," he said again. I read about the Arcturians, and many have said that they are highly evolved spiritual beings. Famous psychic Edgar Cayce (1877-1945) wrote about them. He was known as the sleeping prophet and the father of holistic medicine. He may have been the most well-documented psychic of the twentieth century. Edgar Cayce was reported to have said that "Arcturus is the highest civilization in our galaxy." But who are they? Purportedly, the Arcturians are an alien race that comes from a planet orbiting Arcturus in the Boötes constellation 36 light-years from Earth. Arcturians are said to be inter-dimensional beings. I asked Anzar why the written information I have read about Arcturians and their origins disagrees with his telling me that he was from Rigel in the Orion constellation.

He told me that "Although I am Arcturian I am from Rigel and Orion." Some have said that Arcturians have protected the Earth from other aliens and want to help with our spiritual development.

So, could it be that I'm of alien origin? In a way, I guess I always suspected that because I've never quite fit in anywhere and have always been very independent. After Christmas 2018, I spoke to Anzar again.

"Anzar, are you there?" I asked.

"Yes. Compatibility," he said.

"What do you mean?"

"Your friends, compatible, and important."

"I agree. Are you saying we have a special connection?" I asked.

"Yes," he said. I thought for a moment. I knew that my good friend Terry, who had been abducted, had Rh-negative blood. O negative to be exact.

"Are Rh negative people the descendants of aliens?"

"Yes," he said. I became frightened thinking about abduction and what happened to Terry.

"How can we protect ourselves?" I asked.

"Your belief and acceptance of the one Consciousness, God, the Creator, and tapping into the one Consciousness, that's what will help you."

"Thank you. Can you give me any more advice?"

"When you see what is not there, you will see what is there," he said.

This statement by Anzar made me think. I sometimes see the air, the molecules in the air moving. Anzar read my mind and answered.

"Yes. You have seen it as a child. What you are told not to see is what you should see," he said.

I've always thought that children are very psychic and then society and our social institutions convince us not to use these God-given abilities.

The day before New Year's Eve 2018, I had another chance to speak to Anzar.

"When I asked which alien race you are, I thought you said Assyrian," I said.

"Sirian," he corrected me.

"But then you said Arcturian? Which one is it?"

"Combination."

Oh, so now I understood. He is of both Sirian and Arcturian extraction and came from Rigel in Orion. Multi-ethnic, multi-planetary. I got it. "The illustration of you that I drew in 1997 and that will appear in *Timeless Deja Vu*, is that correct?"

"It is one of my appearances, been around a long time." I thought for a moment.

"Am I getting just little bits of information at a time so as not to overwhelm me?" I asked.

"Yes. There is much more."

"When will the reveal be?"

"Soon, more than likely, depends. It may lead to assassinations." Then it dawned on me, something that I had been thinking for a long time.

"Is that what happened to JFK and RFK?"

"Yes, because they would reveal info about aliens."

"MLK?"

"Yes and no."

"What?" He didn't answer.

"Trust your connection. Flow with it, like a stream, let the great Consciousness flow." Talking to Anzar, I felt confident that I would be successful and keep growing my knowledge and wisdom in order to help people.

On January 8, 2019, I spoke with Anzar the Progenitor again.

"Thank you for speaking with me. I'm trying to help people. Am I on the right track with my thinking? Is the spiritual/quantum realm the same realm aliens utilize for transport and contact? How do I transport myself?" I asked.

"You can go back or forward in time or travel great distances. Remote viewing, it can be done. Study that."

A few days later I asked Anzar: "These signals, Fast Radio Bursts (FRB), is this what you meant by an audible sign from aliens?"

"Yes."

"And the visual is coming?"

"Yes. Prepare, acknowledge, secure, and protect," he said.

"What more can I do to enhance my abilities to help people?"

"Embrace, endeavor, let go of fear, fearless living." I had a lot to think about. I believe I was approaching what the famous conspiracy theorist and writer Jim Marrs called, "the boggle point." That is the point where you simply cannot fathom or process what you are being told.

A few days later I had more questions for Anzar.

"This idea of time travel…you said it is totally possible in the spirit realm that you operate in. So, if I get into the meditative state, I can travel in time?"

"Yes."

"And just to confirm, the audible signal you told me about is the FRBs that are coming in now?"

"Yes."

"And that is the beginning of the big reveal?"

"Yes."

"And the visual will come next?"

"Yes."

"Will I be part of the visual?"

"Yes." Oh, great, what does that mean. I was too overwhelmed to dig deeper, so I let it go.

"I really appreciate you talking to me," I said.

"Let the light envelop you, and it will carry you throughout time and space. That is the key. The master key."

Then another voice entered my head, but I wasn't sure if it was from Anzar, but it sounded like him.

"There is here and here is there," said the voice. I think the speaker was referring to non-locality.

"I think I understand," I said.

"The light is your salvation, the light is the truth, the light is your destiny, blessed is the light," said Anzar as the communication ended.

I remembered what my spirit guide Theodora had told me: "Stay in the light, feel the light, be the light." And the connections continue dear readers. I've come to believe that we need to balance ourselves somewhere between complacency and hysteria as we deal with whatever is coming. Be prepared, and our lives and learning will continue on, forever.

EPILOGUE

As we come to the end of this second *Timeless* book, I'm thinking of all the people who have taught me over the years: my school teachers, sergeants and officers in the army, college professors, bosses, Ginger, family, friends, enemies, and even random strangers. Everyone has taught me something, my mom and dad most of all. I wouldn't be writing this book if it wasn't for my mom and her interest in the magical realm. My dad taught me practical things. He showed me the proper way to hold and swing a hammer. This combination of the mystical and practical has made me who I am today. I remember, when I was a young boy and we visited the Washington State Fair in Puyallup, a Native American man told me not to drag my feet or clomp around when I walk.

"Walk quietly, gently, respectfully, and with purpose upon the Earth," he said. I didn't understand the whole meaning then, but I do now. My walking meditation wherein I can communicate with those who have passed on is the fulfillment of that prophecy. I've developed my natural gift as a medium through focused calm on these daily walks. It's an awesome responsibility to speak with those who inhabit the spirit world. Most of them desperately want to connect with their loved ones whom they left behind. I help them, it's my duty, my mission, and I'm both humbled and honored by being able to serve as a bridge between this world the next. When I think of how I felt comfortable in graveyards as a young boy when others my age (and most people) didn't, it all makes sense. It was a sign. An older Norwegian lady named Kari who was a friend of my mom and dad's, used to have me form a bridge with my hand when I was a kid. It was our tradition. She had lost her children long before I was born, so she passed this ritual on to me. She would raise her hand up, palm down, and smile broadly as my mom and dad and the other Norwegian immigrants in their circle of friends watched.

"Can you remember, to build the bridge?" I would make the bridge with her not knowing the significance of what I was doing. Now I know. I'm a bridge builder. It was my destiny.

A sailor named Jose, whom I met while we were visiting my Uncle Thorvald's oil tanker docked in Vancouver, British Columbia, told me to remain calm and not to make a face when I lifted something heavy or used maximum effort when working.

"Control your emotions. You lose strength when you make a face," he said. He was from Venezuela, but I only knew his first name. Later I told Uncle Thorvald that I would travel to Venezuela someday to find Jose. He laughed at that notion. I also remember that while I was hanging out with Jose and the other sailors, I watched a film they were showing about East Indian fakirs and mystics who could pierce their bodies in various places without harm and without much bleeding. I was fascinated. When someone put a new film in that showed naked women, Jose quickly spirited me out of the room.

"You idiot! His uncle is the captain," he said to the projectionist. He reinforced the idea that focused calm brings your greatest strength.

I've told nearly every story of every paranormal experience that I've had. Some things remain in my head, so I'm not discounting the idea of a third book, in fact, it's already in the works. My understanding of previous experiences continues to deepen. For instance, in the first *Timeless* book I wrote about the special connection my mother and my brother had while he was facing death in the Vietnam War. Their connection makes every bit of sense in the quantum realm. Also, regarding the story about Willy whom I encountered in my trip to Barrow, Alaska, I've re-examined who Willy really is, and I now believe that he was a ghost and a spirit guide. It makes sense to me now why the Native Alaskans I met there were perplexed and shocked when I said I had seen him and spoken to him. I've researched for information about him and there isn't any mention of him in Barrow. Paranormal experiences have continued to happen to me in 2017, 2018, 2019, and I will undoubtedly continue to have them for the rest of my life. The primary goal of these books has been to inspire others to share their experiences and work with and support scientists like Dean Radin from the Institute of Noetic Sciences (IONS) who continue their psi (psychic) research. Maybe a clue to the answer we're all searching for was best expressed by my dear departed friend Gene Thorkildsen who told me after his death, "It's all true!"

I don't know the definitive answer to the big question of what happens after death, but I have an idea. I believe that we exist simultaneously along with other beings in many different dimensions. Some beings can cross over to other dimensions, we may also, maybe even without knowing that we are. Sometimes the dimensions intercept and converge, past and present, and future together. This convergence and interception could help explain ghosts, hauntings, deja vu, precognition, and all the other paranormal phenomena. Some people can glimpse these things and peek into other dimensions. Maybe we don't die, we just continue in either new identities (reincarnation) or as ourselves but with divergent outcomes in alternative dimensions, never missing a beat.

So, how does the concept of God fit into all this one might ask? I pray every day. My parents taught me to pray, and I've taught my children. Now, some people might think that praying is a waste of time, naïve, foolish, or misguided, but somehow, I don't think so. Praying is a form of mind focus like meditation. Dean Radin, in his book *Supernormal,* wrote about the practice of yoga and meditation and its connection to our inherent supernormal mental powers, such as telepathy, clairvoyance, and precognition. Radin focuses on Patanjali's mysterious Yoga Sutras, which are 2,000-year-old meditation practices believed to release our extraordinary powers. Ancient people were aware of much more than we give them credit for today.

In the movie *Cowboys and Aliens*, a preacher named Meacham says:

"God doesn't care who you were, he only cares about who you are…first you earn his presence, then you acknowledge his presence, then you act on it." Although it wasn't the best movie I've ever seen, some of the dialogue was thought-provoking. I've found that the argument over the existence of God isn't productive. My mom always told me not to discuss religion in a social setting. I understand why, because people can get very upset and then nobody is listening. Let's assume there is no God, just for a moment. How does praying or believing in a higher power hurt anyone? Maybe you can strengthen your resolve by focusing on good things through prayer? We all know that the only reason that good things happen in the world is because good people work very hard to make them happen. If prayer and belief in a higher power can facilitate that process of creating good in the world, then it's certainly a positive practice that should be encouraged. Carl Jung had a Latin inscription carved above the door of his house in Kusnacht, Switzerland: "VOCATUS ATQUE NON VOCATUS DEUS ADERIT." In English, the inscription reads: "Called or not called, God will be present."

In 1992, the eccentric billionaire Ross Perot ran for president. He chose Admiral James Stockdale as his running mate. Admiral Stockdale was a US Navy aviator who earned the Medal of Honor. He was shot down over North Vietnam and held and tortured as a prisoner of war (POW) for seven years in the infamous Hanoi Hilton. I admired him greatly and found this quote, the foundation of what has come to be known as the Stockdale Paradox, to be very insightful.

"You must never confuse faith that you will prevail in the end—which you can never afford to lose—with the discipline to confront the most brutal facts of your current reality, whatever they might be." So, in other words, you must combine faith and realism through experience. A wise man.

In closing, I wanted to share this quote from one of my favorite authors, Ray Bradbury: "In my later years I have looked in the mirror each day and found a happy person staring back. Occasionally I wonder why I can be so happy. The answer is that every day of my life I've worked only for myself and for the joy that comes from writing and creating. The image in my mirror is not optimistic, but the result of optimal behavior." Maybe this is the key to a good life.

I've thought of this optimal behavior idea a great deal. We spend one-third of our life sleeping, one-third at work, and one-third at home, commuting, out and about with friends and loved ones, and other activities. Since one-third of our life is spent at work, it stands to reason that we should pursue a career that is both fulfilling and rewarding. If you like your job, you'll likely be good at that job and serve as an inspiration to others. The opposite is also true. The one-third we spend sleeping is essential for good health and for dreaming which can be up to 25 percent of our time asleep. Carl Jung believed that the unconscious mind was at work while a person was dreaming. He thought that dreams provided a view of the subconscious and helped dreamers understand their conscious lives. Dreams allow a dialogue between the conscious and subconscious.

In my view, we're dream beings, and those dreams can help us achieve optimal behavior and live better and happier lives. Doctors have noted that brain activity continues long after clinical death is declared. These delta wave bursts recorded after a patient has been declared clinically dead are associated with deep REM sleep and dreaming. What can we make of this? There is life after life and reason to be hopeful and encouraged. Optimal behavior, based on the combination of faith and realism through experience that Admiral Stockdale wrote about, is an excellent concept for a life of meaning and fulfillment.

My mother came to me in a vision in 2014. She told me that there are many paths to God, and then she began choking. I tried to help her and did the Heimlich maneuver, but she was frozen solid like a statue. It was frightening, but instructive. I believe that it's extremely difficult for those who have passed on to communicate with us and it's extremely difficult for us to receive their communication. It takes maximum effort. My mom's imparted wisdom from the afterlife was in keeping with her philosophy in life—believe in God, be kind, be smart, be strong, and work hard. I know it wasn't easy for my parents living under Nazi occupation in World War II, losing a child during the war, and coming to America with no money and very little formal education. I witnessed how some people treated my parents because of their foreign accents and broken English. Whenever I hear people making fun of someone because of their foreign accent, I ask them: "How many languages do you speak?"

I remember when we went with my parents to a tree farm in Marysville, Washington, in 1987. My eldest sons Bjørn and Byron were with me. It was a fun outing with my parents. We drove separately, and as we were walking out, I was standing next to my mom and dad's car. They didn't know which way to turn and they asked the tree farm attendant. My dad made a joke with him, and the guy went into his stupid, degrading Swedish Chef impression. My mom hit my dad's arm.

"See, that's what you get," said my mom. My dad's thick accent prompted the ridicule. I felt sorry for dad. My parents encouraged me to learn Norwegian but didn't want me to speak it very much. They didn't want me to have an accent. My mom once said that she felt that she and dad were lucky because all they had to do not to be treated poorly was to remain silent and keep smiling. For people of color, they can't hide or disguise themselves. She knew this and understood.

Because of my unique abilities, I've been able to see and talk with my parents since they have passed on. If not, I would be sad and lonely without them. I keep them alive in my memories and through my occasional paranormal encounters. I wrote a poem about missing my parents entitled "Dream of the Sea." I wrote it in Norwegian first, because that is how it came to me, then translated it into English.

Dream of the Sea

It comes as an adventure,

with sorrow, possibility,

and finality.

Sunrise sailor,

sunset mariner,

both born and borne by the sea,

refugee, New World,

life and death, home again,

mountain rest, sea breeze.

Long out into the ocean,

where sky meets water,

where sun lies down at night,

mother and father,

in a dream of the sea.

Writing and speaking about my parents helps me to realize that they're not gone. I believe that since we're open to other dimensions, we can see both the future and the past because the present is merely an illusion as we move through time and space. There may be an infinite number of ways in which our consciousness exists, not just embodied in human form. We may also be incorporating what we've learned from others into our consciousness as it evolves or tap into what Carl Jung called the collective unconscious. Dean Radin writes in his book *Real Magic* that three fundamental ideas have emerged from the esoteric cosmologies that produced all religious traditions:

1. Consciousness is fundamental.

2. Everything is interconnected.

3. There is only one consciousness.

These three ideas are the basis of psi, the paranormal, and what we call real magic. There is a correlation between what scientists like Dean Radin are studying and what mystics have been doing for millennia. In a book entitled *The Science of Enlightenment*, by Shinzen Young, the author provides the reader with a comprehensive overview of meditation traditions around the world, offers some practical advice, and connects the dots for the western mind. He identifies three realms of consciousness:

1. The everyday realm of consciousness.

2. The intermediate realm of consciousness.

3. The Source, the Divine, or God.

It's in the intermediate realm (the alpha brain wave state) that experienced meditators can encounter paranormal or psi phenomena. Most meditation traditions advise people to not become overly enraptured by the phenomena and instead keep pushing to the source in order to be truly enlightened.

I've decided that the near-death experiences I've had (like my Alaska experience in this book and my Deception Pass experience in the first book), forks in the road of time, are alternate life experiences (ALEs). ALEs are where we die in one world or dimension and continue to live in another, but not as another person or entity like in reincarnation, but as ourselves, as if the death didn't occur. I'm convinced this has happened several times to me. Maybe I'm like a cat with nine lives. This tradition may have come from China. The number nine is a magical number in many different cultures around the world. It's the trinity of trinities. Well, a few more ALEs and then we'll see.

To summarize, from my life journey of discovery, I've learned to swing a hammer of truth in a magical realm while I walk gently and purposefully on the Earth, control my emotions through focused calmness, conserve my energy, and serve as a bridge between the physical and spiritual worlds. Through my research of quantum physics, I've learned that the spirit world is the quantum world and that we're on the cusp of a major paradigm shift of understanding and acceptance of the paranormal. I must help people on their journey of discovery guided by the advice my spirit friends Maia and Gene gave me: Experiencing is believing and believing is experiencing.

Since I was little, I've always thought we were part of a larger whole. As Tom Joad said in John Steinbeck's novel, *Grapes of Wrath*: "A fellow ain't got a soul of his own, just little piece of a big soul, the one big soul that belongs to everybody." When I came home from the Army in 1982, the house that I grew up in felt smaller than I remembered it being. Was it because I had grown larger? Had the experience of the military caused me to see the world as a man instead of a boy? Had my construction of reality changed? I'm not sure. Your home is part of who you are. We feel nostalgic about where we grew up and the experiences that went with the place. Sigmund Freud believed that any dream about a house is a dream about one's own soul or self. When you think about it, we interact with the place, and the place interacts with us. Our home is part of us. In other words, home is not just where you live, it's who you are. It's not surprising then that ghosts haunt the places where they lived and spent most of their time. It's also not surprising then that we all share the yearning to go back home, to the location, to our dreams, and to the memories where all the clues to our journey reside. We can, and we will, because we're timeless.

ABOUT THE AUTHOR

Bruce Olav Solheim was born on September 3, 1958, in Seattle, Washington, to hard-working Norwegian immigrant parents, Asbjørn and Olaug Solheim. Bruce was the first person in his family to go to college. He served for six years in the US Army as a jail guard and later as a helicopter pilot. He earned his PhD in history from Bowling Green State University in 1993.

Bruce is currently a distinguished professor of history at Citrus College in Glendora, California. He also served as a Fulbright Professor in 2003 at the University of Tromsø in northern Norway.

Bruce founded the Veterans Program at Citrus College and cofounded, with Manuel Martinez and Ginger De Villa-Rose, the Boots to Books transition course—the first college course in the United States designed specifically for recently returned veterans. He has published eight books and has written ten plays, two of which have been produced.

Bruce is married to Ginger, the girl of his dreams, who is a professional helicopter pilot and certified flight instructor. He has been blessed with four wonderful children: Bjørn, Byron, Caitlin, and Leif. He also has a precious grandson, Liam. Bruce, his brother, and his two nephews still own the family home in Åse, Norway, two hundred miles above the Arctic Circle.

ABOUT THE ARTIST

Gary Dumm is a life-long Cleveland resident and artist who worked with Harvey Pekar on *American Splendor* since Pekar began self-publishing that comic 42 years ago. He has shown artwork in exhibitions nationally from Cleveland to San Francisco and internationally from Canada to Germany. His cartoons have been shown in *Entertainment Weekly*, the *New York Times*, the *Village Voice* and France's *le Monde* and in *Cleveland Scene, Free Times* and *Plain Dealer*.

Currently, Gary writes and draws pieces for *Music Makers Rag* (biographies of blues musicians helped by that organization out of North Carolina) and juggles several graphic novel projects. His talented wife, Laura, adds color to his work as required, allowing him to do that much more in black and white. You can learn more about Gary and Laura's art at: https://www.dummart.com/.

The first Timeless book is available on Amazon. Timeless: A Paranormal Personal History by Bruce Olav Solheim, Ph.D. ISBN: 978-1721140848

Dr. Bruce has his own monthly radio show. Timeless Esoterica. The show deals with the paranormal, supernatural, conspiracies, hidden history, and oddities. You can find more information at: http://artistfirst.com/drbruce.htm.

Dr. Bruce teaches a Paranormal Personal History course at Citrus College. Please contact the Citrus College Continuing Education Department: http://citruscollege.edu/ce/Pages/ContactUs.aspx. Our you can contact Dr. Bruce at bootstobooks@gmail.com for more information.

You can learn more about Dr. Bruce and his work at www.bruceolavsolheim.com.

CPSIA information can be obtained
at www.ICGtesting.com
Printed in the USA
LVHW041358180222
711325LV00005B/722

9 780578 464466